T0246031

GO HIGHER

GO HIGHER

Life will test you. When you get through that, it's your testimony.

GO HIGHER

Five Practices for Purpose, Success, and Inner Peace

Sean "Big Sean" Anderson

SIMON ELEMENT

New York Amsterdam/Antwerp London Toronto Sydney New Delhi

SIMON
ELEMENT
An Imprint of Simon & Schuster, LLC
1230 Avenue of the Americas
New York, NY 10020

First Simon Element hardcover edition January 2025

For information about special discounts for bulk purchases, please contact Simon & Schuster Special Sales at 1-866-506-1949 or business@simonandschuster.com.

The Simon & Schuster Speakers Bureau can bring authors to your live event. For more information or to book an event, contact the Simon & Schuster Speakers Bureau at 1-866-248-3049 or visit our website at www.simonspeakers.com.

Interior design by Jason Snyder

Manufactured in the United States of America

10 9 8 7 6 5 4 3 2 1

Library of Congress Cataloging-in-Publication Data has been applied for.

ISBN 978-1-6680-4573-2
ISBN 978-1-6680-4575-6 (ebook)

For my younger self, and in honor of
the infinite potential I see in others,
including my son, Noah.

CONTENTS

Foreword

JAY SHETTY

BEFORE I EVER MET SEAN, I'd heard from so many people that "you guys should know each other. You'd really get along." As it turned out, he was hearing the same thing about me; one friend of his who believed in reincarnation swore we were brothers in a past life. Clearly, we were meant to connect.

And, sure enough, when he came on my podcast a few years ago, we wound up having an incredible conversation—so much so that we had to do a part two. To this day, so many people I bump into tell me how powerful an impact those exchanges had on them. Listeners said they cast Sean in a whole new light, and self-help in a new light, too. That's when I first told Sean he should consider writing a book.

I'm thrilled that not only has he written a book but the book is so personal and powerful. You all know Sean for the talented lyricist and rapper that he is; here you'll meet the human behind it all who meditates, journals, and goes to therapy to navigate the ups and downs of life. What he shares is lived experience, tried and tested and what he personally practices. Sean's insights have not only helped him manifest an incredible career and inner peace but also allowed him to feel real joy.

I think there are preconceived notions about both rappers and self-help practitioners. Sean shatters both of those clichés. He shows how actually taking care of your soul and working on yourself are things that are accessible, practical, and relevant to everyone.

As Sean says in the book, he's found himself in a dark place more than once. Working on himself helped him to find success, rise from depression, and become the father he wants to be for Noah. The fact that he's been able to use these positive strategies at so many different points in his life is a testament to their power and impact.

There are so many forces at work pulling us down and bringing us lower. I'm grateful that Sean is using his platform to encourage people to Go Higher—to reach higher ideas, frequencies, relationships, and ways of living. *Go Higher* is full of joy, light, and love—just like my friend Sean.

With love and gratitude,

Jay Shetty
Author, coach, former monk
#1 *New York Times* bestselling author
Host of the *ON Purpose* podcast
Cofounder of Juni Tea
Chief purpose officer at Calm

INTRODUCTION
The Five Practices: Accept, Strategize, Try, Trust, Manifest

WHILE MOST PEOPLE KNOW ME as a successful rapper, the truth is that, above all else, I'm on a path of self-knowledge and spiritual development. And I wouldn't be where I am today if I hadn't discovered ways to take care of myself emotionally and mentally.

I believe that we need to maintain our spiritual health the way that we would our diet, car, or an exercise program. It all goes under the category of taking care of yourself. You need to get oil changes and annual checkups; so, too, you need to spend quiet time looking within yourself, asking hard questions, and finding your path to inner peace.

What if we started doing the work on ourselves before we hit a low point? What if we treated our spiritual health the same way we did our physical and financial health? What if we made it part of our daily lives? There's no wrong time to start your journey of self-improvement. If you can do the work proactively, you'll be in a much better situation when you run into difficult times, as we all do. It's a lot easier to become stronger when you're not in crisis. What I mean by crisis is when you have your back against the wall and everything's going wrong. You can still do that self-work then, but it's easier when you're coming from a place of strength. And, by the way, this isn't "work" the way a day job is work. It doesn't take energy—it gives energy.

I've spent years honing my skills of self-reflection: meditation, journaling, and therapy. To become better at all these techniques, I've met with countless spiritual leaders and studied books like *The Seven Spiritual Laws of Success*, *The Four Agreements*, and *Ask and It Is Given*. I've done Dave Asprey's 40 Years of Zen program. I know not everyone has time to do the deep dives I've done, so I'm here to share my favorite lessons and how they've helped me on my quest to become stronger.

I've always wanted to write a book. When I sat down and tried to figure out how to talk about what can feel like pretty out-there topics, I asked myself: *As a student of self-knowledge, what could I contribute to the conversation that might feel new?* Looking back on my life and the work I've done, I realized that everything that's worked for me could be boiled down into five practices: **accept, strategize, try, trust,** and **manifest**.

Most of the experiences that I've learned from and that have helped me become my best self clearly demonstrate one or more of these five ideas. In this book, I'll tell stories from my life that I hope will illustrate the ways in which these practices have played out. You'll see relevant practices listed below the title of each chapter, and you'll see some of my related song lyrics, too. These aren't steps where you finish one and then move on to the next. As you'll see throughout the book, each practice is meant to be part of an ongoing process of learning about yourself and always going higher.

I learned all of this the hard way. When I was in high school, I met

Kanye West. After months of sending me beats that I would work on and send back to him, he said he wanted to sign me.

What the fuck? I was a nobody! I was seventeen! Still in high school! This was my number one favorite artist at the time! He wanted to work with me? Getting signed was my ultimate goal, and here it was!

That was like the poster on my wall coming to life. When that happened, I figured my life was made, you know? I was beyond ecstatic. I was thinking my dreams had been answered . . .

Then I didn't hear from him for almost two years. That situation led to my first bout of depression. I didn't want to kill myself, but it was bad. The more time went by, the more I felt like I was in quicksand, sinking deeper and deeper. I felt worthless. I felt like I'd failed and let everyone down. My thought wasn't that I wanted to die exactly—I was just *over it*. I thought, *I don't want to deal with this shit anymore.*

In hindsight, these were growing pains that shaped my character. Growing pains can make you a greater version of yourself. Always keep that in mind when you're going through a tough situation and you feel like things aren't going your way. It's all temporary.

God got me through that. My family got me through that. More than anything, doing the work on myself got me through that. When I was younger, we went to church every Sunday. I was taught to accept that there was more to life than we could see. And I've experienced so many miracles. I've dodged figurative and literal bullets and beaten the odds by a billion. I've been saved by love and dedication.

Part of why I rap about it now is because not everyone has unconditional love in their life like I had from my parents and my brother. I want everyone to know that you can always turn things around and find inside yourself whatever love you don't have from others. I make music for people who can relate to what I'm saying. I focus on that and don't pay attention to the other stuff. The game is always changing, and there's no point in focusing on what you can't change.

Pulling myself out of my darkest moments took real work—and every situation was different and required different tools. As I said, I see that work as being in five parts. I'm sharing them here for whoever wants to do that work, whether they're struggling or just want to get to the next level.

Here's how I've applied the five practices in my life: I learned how to **accept** the situation I was in, **strategize** a way out of it, **try** every day to do the best work I could, **trust** my instincts and that the right people would appear in my life, and get myself into the right headspace to let me **manifest** a beautiful future. I realized that being inspired and inspiring others—through music or any other means I could—was the most important thing to me.

When I was coming up, I would hear artists talk about loss or depression, but never what to do about it. I'm not saying that wasn't there, but in my world, I wasn't seeing it. I make songs and write about these things in the hope that there are other people out there now who might need it, too. Again and again in my life, I've seen how talking about problems has helped solve them. Communication is the bridge to salvation.

I enjoy success today because, when I was struggling, I shared what I was going through, refused to give up on myself, and took my healing seriously. My goal is to encourage others to do the same in their own way.

I just became a father for the first time. Part of my goal in writing this book now is that I want my son, Noah, to grow up in a world that values mental and emotional well-being and the work that goes into being a whole person.

I've included a glossary of terms to help clarify what I mean when I talk about things like vibration and affirmations, and a list of resources at the back of the book in case you'd like to research these topics further.

I'll also offer journal prompts at the end of each section as a way to help you think through how these practices are already at play in your own life, and how you could become even more intentional about living the life you want to live, whether by offering forgiveness, taking risks, or believing in your own power.

This is a book of reassurance and opportunities. Like all of us, I've been through a lot, and I've found ways to think and act that helped me grow. From this new place of strength, I feel so lucky that I get to share strategies for growth that will give you an advantage in every part of your life and help you expedite your destiny.

Whenever people used to tell me, "Take the time to work on yourself," I'd say, "What time? There is no time to take." The last thing any of us wants to hear is that we have to work harder—especially if you already have two jobs, or a family, or a side hustle. But focusing on your internal well-being will give you more time and more energy. Once you've done the healing work on yourself, everything you want will be possible.

Your purpose is to do what makes you happy, and to do it out of love. If you act in a way that doesn't harm others or come from a bad place, if you do what comes out of genuine love and passion, you're fulfilling your destiny. If you happen to impact others in the process, then that's incredible and an extra bonus. But the judge of how you're doing in life has to always and only be you.

The business of trying to please everybody else is a business you'll never be successful at. Even if you do please everyone, then you have to ask, will *you* be satisfied? Everyone is such a unique person that things apply to some people and don't apply to others. So it's important to focus on what you can control, which is the inner work, without worrying about what will come of it. Express yourself, write your poems, play your instruments, paint your pictures, tell your stories, play your sports, et cetera. Whatever it is you do, there's an art to it. There is an art to being a doctor. There's an art to being a lawyer. There's an art to being a truck driver. There's an art to being a hairdresser. There's an art to raising children and managing a household. Do you, be you, and worry later about the details.

For me, another governing philosophy is *Nothing lasts forever.* Before you even start thinking about whatever you're going through and whether or not you're in crisis right now, I urge you to remember that *it's going to end.* That's what I've learned above all else in dealing with losses and pain: when you know it's temporary, it's possible to survive anything. And everything is temporary.

One practice that's given me peace is acknowledging that it's up to me what energy I bring to my obligations. I can say "I *have* to" or I can say "I *get* to." I used to see everything as a chore, one more demand on my time. Now I see each task as something that I'm allowed to do. I get to wake up with my baby son in the morning. I get to go into the studio to finish an album. I get to write this book. I don't say "I have to go do this show in Vegas"; I say "I get to go to Vegas to do a show, and even if the schedule is tough, that money opens up space when I'm back from the trip so I can focus on writing a book and making an album."

I'm aware that some of these situations are unique to my life as a performer, but the point is, we all have responsibilities in life. Changing your perspective can make it so much easier to fulfill them. It only takes seconds to adopt a more positive outlook, but it can be a make-or-break moment for your sanity and productivity.

This isn't going to be complicated. It shouldn't feel like homework. Yes, when you're present in your own life, you're going to have to uncover and forgive some harsh realities about your damn self. That's hard, but good-hard—the difficult part that pays off, like cleaning your house.

Life is tough, but we get to choose our struggles. Do you prefer the hard work of exercising and eating right to stay fit now or the harder consequences of poor health later? When the result isn't what you want it to be, do you choose to dwell on it or learn from the experience?

In doing this inner work, I had to get familiar with all of the parts of myself. It took a lot of work to understand that I couldn't live my life for others but that I needed to live it for myself. I was getting so much of my validation from outside myself: awards, money, praise. But it was only when I began to validate myself that I started to truly experience a different high. Discipline and consistency are what lead you to greatness. You have to do the hard and uncomfortable inner work in the fierce pursuit of loving yourself and setting boundaries. That's how you achieve true greatness.

Depending on your environment and where you're at in your life, doing work on yourself might not be as hard for you as it is for some of us. You might be at a point where you're so receptive it clicks right away, or you might need to let these things simmer for a while until they reach a boil. There is no such thing as failure, only lessons. You find a reason to keep going, to keep moving forward.

The first stage of working toward growth is understanding where you're starting from. We all start at different places, and everybody hits roadblocks at some point. Some of us start our journey of self-actualization at rock bottom. I hope to inspire you to begin your journey whether you're struggling or thriving.

Writing this book is the next step on my journey as an advocate for introspection and taking care of every part of yourself (physical, mental, emotional, and spiritual). Besides it being a lifelong goal of mine, I especially wanted to do this book because I felt an absence of conversations around the emotional well-being of black men and people of color.

Here's a question I like to ask people: *What's your life's purpose, and how did you find it?* I think people get the idea of "purpose" wrong sometimes. They think it needs to be something you blast to the world to show you're making a difference. But I've come to realize that making a difference in yourself—just in your own life—is already changing the world.

Self-care is not selfish. If you're happy with the way you are, or even if you've accepted the way you are, you are working to improve this greater consciousness. As you become "better," whatever that may mean for you, that helps the people around you become more conscious of themselves and aware of their own potential.

The world, especially the Western world, has taught us to believe that we exist as individuals and nothing more, but the truth is that we are all part of some kind of collective, family, or team. We are all interconnected. In a family, you can be the family member who is weighing the rest of the family down, or you can be the family member who is helping everyone—the way my grandmother did by creating a haven for us in her home.

If we can make self-work part of our daily routine, then when we go through tough times, we will already have the armor and the tools to recover. It's about figuring out your version of success, which might have nothing to do with a career or money.

Not everyone is on the same frequency as me, so not everyone is going to like me or what I do. The point of life isn't to get everyone to like you. Again, no one has ever been successful in the business of pleasing everybody. I've realized that, for me, the point of being a creative person is to express myself and to do it with dignity and confidence, and to make something I'm proud of. And those are things that are totally within my own control. Each of us has our own goals, and with the help of these five practices, each of us can go higher.

THE FIVE PRACTICES

I. Accept

One of the most important things to do in life is to **accept** your fate as it's been revealed to you up to this point: who you are, what you have, what you've done so far. You're not living in a dream world or in denial. You're **accepting** yourself, your desires, your background, your talents, and your faults. You're **accepting** the world you live in as it is and not obsessing over how you wish it could be. You might have to **accept** that what you want and what society seems to want for you could be at odds, or you might have to **accept** that society could be wrong in how it's viewed you until now. And you're **accepting** that everything can change at any time.

Acceptance means seeing clearly where you are right now and also acknowledging that you have the power to change any situation that you're in, no matter how possible or impossible other people say that is. We have the power of a whole universe inside of us. There's a parallel between the cells in our body and the stars in the sky.

When you face the reality of how things are, when you see it all clearly and without shame or regret, that's when you become ready for change. That's when you can start asking new questions, like "Are you satisfied with where you are?" If you're a person who knows you're made for more than what you're experiencing now, that you're made to do something that fulfills you more, then once you've done the work of **acceptance**, it's time to figure out what that bigger thing is and how to do it. But you have to **accept** reality first.

Part of **acceptance** is appreciating what you have before you think about what you'd like to change. That's what makes the next gift possible—it may be something you can't even imagine yet. But at least when you **accept** what's come before, you're opening up space for new information to present itself.

II. Strategize

One of my favorite questions to ask is "How could it get any better than this?" If you feel that you're in what you would consider an ideal situation—which is not how the majority of us feel at any given time—ask yourself: How can it improve? What else is possible? If there is already a ceiling, how do you go through the roof? There are no limits to how much the universe loves you. There is always more to offer if you desire it. And there's enough for all of us.

There are so many different ways that humans **strategize**. Some of us research things on the internet; some of us have mentors who can help us. Personally, when I **strategize**, the first thing I ask myself is "How can I expedite this thing that I believe is destined to happen? Who can help me go higher?"

It's also important when you're **strategizing** that you see what works best for you. Some people are more analytical and love digging through articles. Some are more sensory and have to go out and experience things firsthand. There are so many ways to **strategize**. See which one works best for you. This isn't school; this is your life.

You may not have the answer, which is okay. To me, when you're putting the energy of *How can I?* into something, it's almost like talking to God or the universe, saying, "Hey, I'm asking for your help now. How can I accomplish this?"

And once you do that, you're in a place to actually put together a plan, with to-do lists and action-oriented goals for making that plan a reality. One thing to remember when you ask the universe for help is that the help may come in a way that you least expect it, or it may come in the form of being able to empower yourself.

III. Try

This is where a lot of people who have big dreams fall off. They have an idea that they're going to **try** something and be great at it immediately, but that almost never happens. You have to **try** and **try** and **try** some more to get really good.

Yes, I have a lyric about doing rather than trying: "Fuck trying and not doing because not doing is something that I'm not doing." I acknowledge that *doing* is the key thing, but I feel like you have to **try** first.

Einstein said, "You never fail until you stop **trying**." Someone somewhere could probably pick up a basketball and be a revolutionary player starting with their first shot, but most people, including Michael Jordan, had to work hard. We all know the story about how Jordan got cut from his high school team before he became the greatest player of all time.

When you see someone performing at a talent show or opening up at a concert or picking up a basketball or studying for a degree, that's **trying**, and we need to respect the effort regardless of the results. We have to be aware that all of us on this plane of existence are trying in some way, shape, or form, even if it's just by waking up to face the day.

Back when I first started to have the courage to **try**, I would show up to open mics, lunchroom rap-battles, and talent shows. I'd perform every chance I could get to show what I had and to sharpen my sword, no matter how big or small the venue. I'd show up even as a last-minute sub without letting it hurt my pride that I hadn't been asked first. I just wanted as many chances as possible to improve.

Occasionally, I'd have some good luck. A friend would say, "I know somebody who knows somebody who has a connection at a studio."

Why did that happen? Because I put myself out there. When you're **trying**, the universe respects it and shows up to help you on your way.

IV. Trust

Right in the middle of **trust** is the letter "u"—and that's the main person you have to **trust**: yourself. Now, I've experienced situations where I **trusted** other people more than I **trusted** myself. There are times when it actually worked out. But sometimes I listened to other people's advice and it was a mistake. When it didn't go well and it wasn't my own idea, that hurt so much more. I felt that I had failed in the situation and failed to listen to my own better judgment. But one of the questions that made me ask was "What is more important to you—listening to yourself or accepting that if you listen to other people you're going to feel terrible?"

Trusting yourself is like working out any other muscle. The more you **trust** your instincts, the more you learn to take what other people say with a grain of salt. Then it's always your own decision, even when you listen to others. Even if you make mistakes, it's still better when you're being true to yourself. You can say, "At least I stood up for my own belief." That's a win on its own.

If you don't **trust** yourself, then you have to ask yourself why that is. Do you think you're not good enough? Do you think you don't deserve to get what you want? Are there ideas you may have inherited that are making you think this way? Have you become a self-sabotager? Is a lack of faith holding you back?

Trust is one of the hardest things to maintain because it gets tested all the time by the world and all the experiences that come with it. But I'm here to tell you that we all have the willpower to make anything we desire happen. I want people to realize that: you must **trust** yourself, and you must **trust** the universe, too.

V. Manifest

Have you ever been on a road and noticed how everyone is moving in time with one another? We move in synchronicity, like cells in a body. When I'm driving on the freeway, I always notice the patterns: white lights coming toward me, red lights going away, like white blood cells and red blood cells, as though I'm in the middle of a vein. As I look around, I see so many signs of our interconnectedness and harmony. The key thing is learning how to be part of that flow without fighting against it.

Once you're more in alignment and more intentional with your energy, you begin to **manifest** your goals. It doesn't always happen on your terms. God gives you what you need more than what you want. Sometimes what you want is what you need, and sometimes what you don't want is what you need. You don't realize that until after you've made it to the other side of whatever it is you're going through. But I believe the universe has a plan for us and that when we're vibrating at the right frequency, we'll be able to attract what we need.

When I decided that I wanted to be a rapper, I ended up meeting some people on my block who rapped. It was like we were magnetically drawn to one another. You start attracting the right people in your life when you're intentional with your energy. It's like tuning the radio to the right station.

GLOSSARY

In this book, I use some terms people might not be familiar with. Here are definitions for a few words you might encounter.

Affirmations are like daily pep talks. I say or write mine in my journal every day. They could be something as simple as one of the following: *I have everything I need to face this day. I am peaceful. I am happy. I am grateful. I am limitless. I am unstoppable.*

Agreements are deals that you make between yourself and the universe. Unlike affirmations, you don't need to renew these every day. They're more like New Year's resolutions that you can update as needed. An example might be "I am present for my family" or "I am making music that I can be proud of."

Ego refers to the conscious part of yourself. This is your public image, your sense of pride, your ambition. If you don't do the inner work that balances the ego with the soul, this is the part of you that will run the show and can get you in trouble.

God/universe/source energy are terms I use interchangeably. I acknowledge that different religions use names like Allah, Yahweh, and Brahman, and while respecting everyone's beliefs, I hope to talk about a universal divine energy that we can all encounter outside of any particular religion or belief system.

Journaling is simply writing in a notebook, whether once a day or once a week or a dozen times a day. Some people I know carry their notebooks everywhere to write down thoughts or lyrics or interesting things people say. Others keep them by their bed and write down their dreams first thing in the morning. Some use a standard composition notebook; others buy fancy leather journals. There's no wrong way to do it.

Manifestation is when you're able to call things forth into being—for me, that's by means of some combination of the work associated with these five practices. I feel I've **manifested** so much of the good in my life by means of my affirmations, agreements, meditation, and other inner work.

Meditation, as I practice it, involves sitting calmly in a place where I feel safe, breathing deeply, and visualizing colored light flowing over and through me. But there are many ways to meditate. It's about taking time out for yourself to clear your mind, even if it's just five minutes a day.

Soul/spirit/higher self are terms I use interchangeably to refer to the core part of us that isn't conscious, like the ego, but that connects to the universe and is nourished by the work of these five practices.

Therapy, also called psychotherapy, talk therapy, or counseling, is going to a professional therapist, usually once a week (though I know people who go twice a week or twice a month) to talk through what's on your mind. Sessions usually last fifty minutes; some therapists see patients in person at an office, and others do it on Zoom. There's solo therapy as well as couples or family therapy, so whether you're working on yourself or on a relationship with a partner or a child, there's someone out there to help you.

Vibration is the energy you're putting out into the world, how you're showing up for life, and the energy you're attaching to. I believe we can sense one another's vibration, and that "vibing" with someone means matching their vibration.

Vision boards are collections of images and statements that you're in the process of transforming from dreams, ideas, and goals into reality. Some people make collages or drawings in their journals. I think of a vision board like a checklist. When I achieve something, I take it off my vision board to make room for something new.

CHAPTER ONE
Finding My Calling

▪ *accepting, trusting, trying*

THE FIRST TIME I WROTE a rap, I was eleven years old and living in Detroit on a street called Northlawn. I lived at the end of the block, and at the beginning of the block, I had two friends who were cousins who had started a rap group. We were down the street at their house one day when they started to tell me that they'd formed a group. And one of them said, "Man, you should be in it."

Eleven-year-old me, not knowing anything about being in a rap group or that it would change the direction of my entire life, was like, *Okay!*

I said I'd join. Then, when it was time to write a rap, I realized that I didn't know what I was doing. I was a huge fan of the Notorious B.I.G., Eminem, Jay-Z, Tupac, Snoop Dogg, Dr. Dre, Bone Thugs-n-Harmony, Nas, Fabolous, and DMX, but I didn't really know how they did what they did. I started carrying around a long yellow notepad, writing down lines and crossing them out, crumpling up pages, and getting more and more nervous about ever being able to come up with anything good.

Finally, after **trying** for days, I got inspired, and the words flowed. When I was done writing, I made a few changes, and then I looked at the page and thought, *Huh, okay! This is all right. This is something.* But I wasn't sure it was good enough to share with people. I figured I'd test it out on my mom before I showed it to anyone else. I brought my note-book home and asked my mom if I could perform my first rap for her.

When I was done, I looked at her and wondered what she'd say. I had no idea if she liked it or not, if she'd tell me I'd embarrassed myself or tell me I was a genius. I was so nervous that my heart was beating out of my chest like crazy!

"Oh, it's good," she said. "Wow. It's *very* good. You should keep going."

That was such an important moment for me, and so generous of her. At that time, gangster rap ruled the genre, and I knew my mom was not a fan. Whatever I wrote was definitely superficial, talking about Rolexes and girls and driving Benzes and things that I knew absolutely nothing about in real life. A lot of my early raps were me painting a picture of who I wanted to be and how I wanted to live, or at least who I thought I wanted to be and how I thought I wanted to live.

Not only did my mom encourage me but she also gave me my first lesson in **manifesting**. "Just visualize what you want," she said. "If that's rapping, see yourself up on stage!"

That's when I wrote down a dream in my school notebook: to be one of the greatest rappers out of Detroit. And just two years later, in eighth grade, I was voted "Most Likely to Be a Rapper Actually from Detroit."

I'm thankful that at eleven I had enough confidence to try to do something new, even though it was nerve-racking at first, and to try to stake out an identity for myself, to say to the world: *Here I am. This is what I'm trying to do.* I knew, even that young, that becoming a rapper wasn't impossible. Some people got to do it. So that's all the proof I needed.

My friends had a mentor who was a few years older than us, another cousin of theirs, who later on became my mentor, too. His name was Sean Menifee.

Sean Menifee lived about six blocks away, and he had a recording studio in the basement of his house. That was where we recorded our very first songs. He helped us develop our style and become comfortable expressing ourselves in front of a mic. He was business-savvy, open-minded, and creative, and he had a son slightly younger than us.

Sean had to be 6'5" or 6'6". When one of the cousins asked me, "What's your rap name going to be?" Sean Menifee said, "You can't be Lil' Sean, because there's already Lil' Shawn."

I said, "Well, I could be Big Sean."

Everyone started laughing. I was eleven, standing next to a giant man named Sean. I was big in heart, but I was physically the opposite of big. But I figured it worked in the same way it does when big guys get the nickname "Tiny." Plus, Biggie Smalls was my favorite rapper at the time, so I thought that was a cool connection. There weren't a lot of rappers named Big anything, because I guess it was reserved for the legends like Notorious B.I.G., Big Pun, and Big L, and there was some kind of silent agreement about that. But I had the audacity to call myself Big Sean, and it stuck.

I was hopeful that I might become widely known as Big Sean. And yet, I knew that even if I was lucky enough to make it, my family might not approve. They were all college graduates. My mom was a schoolteacher, and my dad was a manager at an airline.

When I decided to be a rapper, I was going against the grain, but luckily, I had a mom who was open-minded enough to feed my dreams and not starve them or tell me that they were delusional. She'd once had her own artistic dream of being an actress. She did commercials, even moved to Manhattan. That's where my brother was born. She'd acted in several national commercials and a number of off-off-Broadway plays.

My parents lived in New York City for a decade. Then my mom tried to move to LA for more acting work. But it was tough. This was during the eighties. There were very few lead roles for Black women. She ended up falling back on her education. (She had a bachelor's degree from the University of Michigan and a master's degree from NYU.)

My mom could have easily shot down my first rap and said, "Don't do that anymore," and I might never have stuck with it. I appreciate her for encouraging me. That was such a monumental moment in my life, her being the first person I rapped for and it going as well as it did.

I came to realize that I am a creative person at heart. I don't travel to every museum in the world and dissect paintings, but on a lot of days, I find ways to get super-inspired. As a kid, I noticed that I loved all music, and as a creator, I loved rap music specifically. I loved how it made me feel. I also loved performing. I loved being in school plays and getting to be a character, delivering lines and entertaining, uplifting, and connecting with people.

That's my story, though. For another person, a different path could be fulfilling. Maybe what you want to do is be a part of a family business. Or maybe you're a teacher and want to innovate in your classroom. It's okay to go against the grain, to be a forward thinker. It's more than okay to listen to yourself, to listen to what makes you happy, even if it's not understood at the time by everyone else around you.

There was a show that took place every week on the main radio station in downtown Detroit, and it was called *Friday Night Cypher*. They would have emcees from around the whole city who would battle rap each other, and the people who won the rounds of each battle rap got to rap on air live every Friday night. It was a show a lot of people tuned into, and you could be heard throughout the whole city because it was on the radio. And I had to be a part of it.

The first time I went to rap on the radio, I was only sixteen. I was so nervous that I messed up. All I could think was, *The whole city is listening*. I couldn't catch the beat properly.

They took me off the mic and went to the next person.

"You can't come back next week," they said.

I was devastated. When I got home, I sat in the dining room crying.

My brother, Brett, tried to comfort me. He said, "It's all good. It's not the end of the world. It's not that big a deal."

I looked at him with anger in my eyes.

"You don't *understand*," I said. "This is what I want to do for *a living*."

I went back the next week, and they let me on, even though they'd said they weren't going to. And I kept showing up, no matter what other obstacles got thrown in my way. One time, my mother begged me not to go to the radio station because there were eight inches of snow on the ground already and it was still coming down. But I couldn't help it; I had to.

I knew early on that I wanted to make music. I had to **accept** that and then do my best to make it happen, while **trusting** that it would work out. It took a long time to figure out how to consistently achieve my dreams, but even way back then, I was driven to **try** to create.

If you don't know your passion, that's totally fine. If you don't have one guiding dream, that's fine, too. **Try** things, see how you feel, pay attention to what your brain and body are telling you. Everyone's mission isn't the same. Sometimes there are people who help others. Sometimes people need to find a path of their own that no one knew existed. And then they wind up leading the rest of us into a new future.

What things do you do best?

What would it take for you to be able to share those talents with the world?

How does it feel seeing yourself do it? Lock onto that feeling. That's you matching the frequency of what you desire, finding your radio station.

If you love yourself,
you'll always be in
good company.

CHAPTER TWO

My Grandmother's Legacy

▪ *accepting, trusting, trying, manifesting*

I GREW UP IN A Motown household. Stevie Wonder, Al Green, Diana Ross, the Jackson 5—that was the music that filled our home. Occasionally, we danced around as a family. We loved one another so much, even though we didn't have it so easy.

When I was just a couple of weeks old, my parents, Myra and James, needed some help financially. They received it from my grandparents—specifically from my mother's mother, Mildred Leonard. Mom, Brett, and I moved from California to live with my grandparents on a prestigious boulevard in Detroit: Outer Drive. That'll mean something to you if you're from Detroit—Marvin Gaye and Motown founder Berry Gordy both used to live on Outer Drive. It was a major accomplishment for my grandparents to have a house there. When I was two years old, my mom and dad split up. I was too little to remember it, but my brother, Brett, was six, and he was pretty upset by it. Brett is handsome, smart, and sweet, plus a super-fast runner. He never tried to be anybody but himself. But he had a harder time with the divorce than I did. It ignited some anger and depression in him. He sometimes raised his voice at my mom or talked from a painful place. He has always been an introspective person and somebody I admire and respect—one of my favorite people in the world. I'm happy I have a brother like him.

My grandfather had a clean style; he wore button-up shirts and had his hair slicked back. He was a very good-looking man. He taught arts and crafts, woodworking, and wood shop, and so he would build a lot of things around the house. I thought he was cool, but my grandma was the *coolest.* She was like one of those women from the movie *Hidden Figures*. A math teacher who could do big sums in her head, she was so good with numbers that it made me feel like she was psychic. She was from West Virginia, but she didn't have the southern sweetness—she had the southern *toughness*. She was the one in our family who did the hardest work.

So many members of my family were discouraged from being themselves and were pushed to fall in line. My dad, who was born and raised in Louisiana, got beaten up for being Black in the wrong place at the wrong time. But in spite of the intense racism that both sides of my family faced, my grandmother became one of the first Black female captains in the U.S. Army during World War II, then later became one of the first female police officers in Detroit, and then a math teacher and counselor at Northwestern High School. She got her bachelor's degree from West Virginia State University and her master's degree from the University of Michigan, where she met my grandfather, who was also working on his master's.

She was the best grandma anyone could ever ask for. She put her heart and more into everything she was involved in, from Sunday dinners to church to giving advice to those who asked her for it. She had a way of making each of us in my family feel special on our birthdays, too, by baking the cakes we loved the most. She gave as much as she could to her family and the world. She made something out of nothing. She supported me in every aspect of my life, even when I went against our family's traditions and pursued my music career instead of going to college. My grandmother helped me become the best version of myself. She was always on me about taking vitamins, working out, and reading as much as I could to become a better man.

She was old-school in all the good ways. She **strategized** so well, approaching everything in a very calculated way, which I saw as a strength. She was thrifty to the extreme. She and my granddad used to wash plastic wrap and aluminum foil to use them again. She put money away for my and my brother's college funds every year. And she and my granddad always paid cash for their new cars. Once they got their first car paid off, they would still put the payments away. Four or five years later, they would have enough money to get a new car. And so they were always able to keep a new car in their driveway.

My grandmother was always helping people out. She let us live with her until we got our own place a couple of miles away, a two-family house on Northlawn Street. We lived in the bottom half of the house, and my grandma's sister-in-law, my auntie, lived in the top. But even then, I would still go to my grandmother's house every day after school.

When I turned sixteen, my grandma gave me her car. It was a bittersweet thing. Yes, it was great to have a car, but it also sucked because the reason I got it was that my strong grandma had had a stroke and had become paralyzed. I felt guilty taking it.

Even through high school, I would go to her house every day for at least a couple of hours. Everyone would meet there: my mom, my grandma, my brother, me. My mom and I would go back to the house on Northlawn for the night, but my brother mostly stayed with my grandma.

It was a hard conversation when I told her I wanted to spend the money she had been saving for me to go to college on making music in a studio. She didn't agree with it, but she still supported me. And that took a lot of understanding from her side. She definitely had her criticisms and made sly remarks sometimes. But she still let me do what I wanted to do without doubting me.

One of the great blessings of my life is that I knew she was proud of me before she passed away. When I bought a house for my mom and her in the Detroit suburbs, she was so moved. That house was a world away from Detroit, even though it wasn't very far in terms of distance. She got to see that her investment in me had paid off. She never saw me perform live, but she did get to see me as a clue on *Jeopardy!*, which was huge for her. And I did play "One Man Can Change the World" for her before she died.

The stroke took half her body away, and maybe some of her mind. A few years later, she became very weak and was in the hospital, where they told us we should say our goodbyes. They unplugged the machines and . . . she didn't die; she rallied. She went on to live several more months. We were so glad she was still around, but there was also agony for her and for the rest of us because she wasn't able to do very much, and we were living with so much uncertainty.

When she did die, I was destroyed. I started punching a wall and busted my hand up. That was a terrible time. Losing her was extremely painful to me because she was my guiding light.

I thought about so many moments when she had stood up for me. My granddaddy, who died when I was in seventh grade, had been very traditional. When I got my ears pierced, he said, "I don't know if I can love a boy with an earring in his ear."

My grandma said, "Oh, stop that! You love Michael Jordan!"

He said, "Michael Jordan's not my grandson!"

He came around eventually, and I think that's mostly because no one could argue with my grandma for long. If you had her on your side, there was no way anyone would ever go against you.

I wish I could have spent more time with my grandaddy and gotten advice from him throughout my life, especially now that I'm a father. I wish I could talk to all my grandparents now. But I **accept** that they're watching over me, and through meditation, I **try** to ask them for advice. I **trust** that when wisdom pops into my head, that's them answering me. I believe some aspect of their spirit is embedded in me. We share the same blood. I feel that on so many levels. With their love and support, I can **manifest** a connection between us and learn from them, even now that they're gone.

Who in your family, alive or dead, do you carry with you? What do they symbolize to you?

In what ways can you make them proud of you? What do you hope to pass on to the ones who come after you?

I spent so many long nights waiting for my day to come.

CHAPTER THREE

Staying Focused

■ *strategizing, trying*

AFTER I GOT MY RAP name at eleven, I became obsessed with the genre. I realized that rapping was my passion, and it was all I thought about. Within a few years, I was known around my city for it. Every Friday after school my senior year, I'd go to the Detroit radio station 102.7 and rap live as part of a show for young emcees, *Friday Night Cypher*. I dreamed of being a Detroit icon. The only local rapper I knew who'd blown up worldwide back then was Eminem—and obviously he was bigger than life; at the time, it felt like he was the most famous person on earth.

When I got that radio gig, I said, "Okay, this is where I'm at now. What's next?" I was **strategizing** the whole time: "If I do well on this show, this is a way that I can get cool with the program directors. So, even if I never get a record deal, I can maybe get my record played on the radio."

I can't overstate the power of establishing yourself locally and making a name for yourself where you're from. This exists in every industry. For me, it was the local radio station where I got experience, made lifelong connections, and met one of my best friends, Mike Posner. But maybe you could intern at a small company near you doing the work you're interested in. This is how you link up with other people doing the same thing and those in your same field who are a bit further along.

I ended up getting my song played on the air because I would do that radio show almost every Friday, and I took it seriously. And that's how I got a big break.

I was a telemarketer at the time. One Saturday, I was in line at the bank waiting to cash my $180 check. The line was out the door, and I knew I'd be there a while.

My cell phone rang. It was my friend Tone. He said, "Kanye's at the station! Yo, man! Go rap for him!"

I looked at the line. I knew I had to cash my check. And I realized that, to catch Kanye, I'd have to leave right that minute. I told Tone I couldn't do it.

He didn't give up. He called our other friend, Brandon, and said, "Sean's gotta go to the station! You should roll down there with him!"

Brandon called me and said, "C'mon! Let's go!"

"I don't have gas money," I said.

"I'll give you twenty dollars for gas to go down there!" Brandon said.

I was nervous, but I couldn't argue with that. On our way there, we stopped off at my house, and I picked up my demo and the press kit I'd made with a photo and a bio.

When we got to the radio station, the receptionist, who knew me from Friday nights, said, "What's up, Sean? What are you doing here on a Saturday?"

Thinking fast, I said, "I think I left my phone back there yesterday. Can I go check the office?"

"Sure, go check real quick," she said. "I think Kanye's back there."

"Really?" I said, hoping I sounded surprised.

I headed back to the offices and saw a DJ I knew.

"Hey, Sean. Kanye's here!" he said.

"Word?"

And then there he was. Kanye West, standing before me.

I can't believe what I'm seeing, I thought. *Holy shit!*

One of the tightest artists on the planet at the time was right there in the radio station.

The DJ introduced us. I shook Kanye's hand.

"I'm a rapper," I said. "And I'm a huge fan of yours."

"Nice to meet you," he said.

"You got time for me to rap for you real quick?" My heart was racing.

"I'm real busy," he said. "I really gotta go."

"Listen," I said, "your song 'Last Call' is my shit. I listen to it all the time on the bus to school." I didn't tell him this, but I'd only ever cried once listening to music, and it was when he told his story at the end of that song on *The College Dropout*.

"Okay," he said. "You can rap while we're walking out."

I was so nervous, but I looked at that moment as life-and-death for me. *I'm either going to do it or I'm not.* I knew that if I did a good job, it could change my life. Because I used to write a new rap every week for that show, I had fifty raps ready. On the way out of the station, I did one after another after another.

I could tell he was feeling me. He looked me right in the eye and raised his eyebrows like, *Oh shit.*

By the time we'd gotten out of the station, a small crowd had gathered around me. My buddy Brandon was there, taking it all in.

Finally, Kanye spoke: "You got a CD?"

I sure did. I handed him that and my press kit.

I had a little charisma, but the real reason I could shine in that environment was because I had done the hard work to be ready for the moment when I could rap for one of my idols. Rapping on the radio was already a lot of pressure. But rapping for Ye was even crazier.

Not only had it gone well; it had gone *great*.

Kanye said, "Come to my listening party for *Late Registration* tonight."

I got the information from his local rep at Def Jam. That night, I was able to hang out with him briefly at the party.

Why was I prepared? Because when I was eleven years old, I put myself in front of a mic. It's so nerve-racking rapping in front of a microphone, but by the time I was sixteen, I was comfortable doing it. Rapping on the radio for a year and a half straight taught me how to rap under pressure.

I had endless new material. I recorded CDs all the time, passed them around school, and sold them for a few dollars. That was the culmination. I felt like from there on my career would be unstoppable. This was the dream made real. I thought I was set for life. When you do things out of passion and love, sometimes it all makes sense later.

When I graduated with a 3.7 GPA from high school, I got offered a full ride to Michigan State University, but I turned it down because I was going to be a rapper. I didn't feel like I could pursue both school and rapping with equal attention, and I needed to follow my heart.

Telling my family I wasn't going to college wasn't easy. College was the way to a better life for my grandmother. She was the first one to go to school in her family, and she was disappointed that I wasn't going to carry on the tradition and go to college, too. She and my granddad were teachers. Then my mom became a teacher. Their family and cousins were all teachers, too.

But my mom knew what it was like to have a dream you didn't get to fully realize, and so she told me, "You should take a shot at it." She agreed that I could always go to college later.

Then . . . nothing happened.

My family understood why I was still at home and not going to school, but I felt an underlying tone of disappointment. All my friends were at college. I was depressed and sleeping in the same twin bed I'd had since I was a kid.

No one felt sorry for me. I had had the fairy-tale rap story where I met Kanye at a radio station and rapped for him. To this day, people think that I just immediately got a record deal, and that's totally not the case. But he was my favorite artist, and I had already made the decision that if I was going to be a rapper for real, that's who I would sign with. It was either him or Eminem for me, or Jay-Z. But G.O.O.D. Music, Kanye's label, felt like it related to me the most, so it was my first choice.

Meeting Kanye was a monumental moment for me. That was one of the first confirmations that I was actually **manifesting** my life. To me, that was proof that we are indeed powerful, energetic beings. I was also still in high school at the time, in my junior year, and Kanye was at a new peak in his career, so he was very, very busy. What was so huge to me was a blip to him.

I kept following up with him, but I was getting no response after he gave me a couple beats to work on. I was sending them back and not really hearing anything for months. There was only very spotty communication between me and his team. I was getting frustrated. This was also the first time I found myself battling depression.

When the contract wasn't coming through, that was the time when I really had to lay my spiritual foundation. I had to have faith in myself that everything would work out; only then could I **manifest** what I wanted. That situation taught me that I had to figure out a way to be proactive. I kept going down to the radio station and rapping every week on Friday nights.

My group, SOS (Sons of the Street), recorded with Sean Menifee. Then, as we got older, we started branching out and recording music in other places—people's houses, basements all over, all sorts of random spots.

We tried so many things to make it. For weeks, my mom and my manager, Carla, would drive us back and forth on the weekends between Detroit and Chicago, about five hours each way, just to record there with someone who supposedly knew someone at Interscope. We spent so much money we didn't have, including whatever room my mom had left on her credit cards. It was exhausting and ultimately didn't lead anywhere except to getting a huge bill from the guy we were recording with and eventually figuring out that he was really using us as a way to get to Ye himself.

But I didn't let any of that stop me because I really believed in myself. I could feel the vibration no matter how down I was, no matter how long I didn't get a hit back from anyone. I always knew that I was preparing for something greater.

I feel like one of the biggest advantages that people who really **manifest** their lives have is that self-acceptance and self-confidence. It's so important to have faith and patience with yourself and to know that it's okay to have moments of weakness. It's okay to cry. It's okay to be frustrated. That's exactly why you've given yourself a foundation of wellness. That's what it's there for.

I knew how bad I wanted to be doing music professionally and wanted to be signed, and it just wasn't happening. So, then I was like, "Okay, let me do some work on myself." I wanted to take parts of myself more seriously.

Really, I had to decide to get it together. Otherwise, I'd have been in a real bad place if a music opportunity ever did come back around. At the time, I'd only read books when I had to for school—*Animal Farm, The Hobbit*. I never read on my own time. But finally I was desperate enough to start reading the books my mother had been telling me to read for a long time.

My mom's self-help books, a bunch of which I'll mention in a list at the end of this book, were key, including *The Four Agreements*, *Ask and It Is Given* by Esther and Jerry Hicks, and *The 48 Laws of Power*. One that really resonated was Deepak Chopra's *The Seven Spiritual Laws of Success*, which argued that success isn't solely the result of hard work, planning, and ambition. Instead, he says that when we understand our true nature, we can learn to live in harmony with natural law and **manifest** our ideal reality. I wound up reading a lot more by Chopra, one of the most famous New Age gurus of all time. He's done so much to bring holistic medicine to the United States.

Using these books of my mom's, I also taught myself to meditate. One of the things that I would do in my meditations was to **try** to attract the people I needed to go higher in my career. That put me in the frame of mind and gave me the positive energy I needed so that when I was presented with opportunities to meet new people, I jumped on them with my whole self.

And then I started attracting people who were producers I didn't know. I started to get my energy back. I kept a journal and meditated. I treated writing and being creative like it was my job—and I'd say it was my job then, too, even if I wasn't getting paid for it yet.

I visualized being on a cliff. My higher self was saying to me that there was an invisible bridge in front of me that was going to take me to the other side. It took a lot of faith to walk over that bridge, but that's what I did. It took four years, but during that time, I never lost faith, and I kept writing. So when my next shot came around, I was ready, and I had a ton of songs.

I was asking the universe at the time to provide me with the people who could help me get to where I needed to be, as well as people I could find a way to help. I wanted it to be a mutually beneficial situation.

I didn't want to be a rapper if it only meant being the biggest star in the world. I was focused on the work, too: I wanted to uplift people. For me, there always has to be a way to bring it back to inspiring people. That's ultimately what I'm here to do and what is fulfilling for me. We all deserve fulfillment.

Just as I started **manifesting** these things, I also started getting back in contact with G.O.O.D. Music, and they became more communicative and started sending me more beats.

Back then, in theory, my best friend and I were a duo. But I was the only one who got to rap for Kanye. I made it clear that I was part of a duo, and all my CDs were with this other guy. But my group member didn't necessarily think like me, and in some ways he was a doubter. This was the first time I experienced the power of having a positive mindset as opposed to a doubting one. It's the difference between asking yourself "What's the worst that can happen?" and "What's the best that can happen?"

Eventually, as communication with the label picked back up, we got word that they only wanted to sign me and not my friend. I thought that this was still good news for both of us in the long run. If it was the other way around, I knew that I would still have been excited. I'd have thought, *He can put me on his first album!* I figured that if either one of us got on, we'd just put the other one on, too.

But the rejection shattered my friend so badly that he wasn't able to get back up. That's one of the moments when he made a choice about how to respond to a disappointment, and that reaction had a huge impact on the rest of his life. When things don't go your way, you can either let it destroy you or you can say to yourself, *Okay, one way or another, this will have been for my greater good. There will be something better coming out of this. Let me take the opportunity and be my best self; put my best foot forward.*

That wasn't how my friend saw it, though. I included him on some of my projects when I first started putting out mixtapes, but his mindset made it so that he sabotaged himself out of having an opportunity with me.

He ended up spiraling. He got arrested, and while he was in jail, he ran into a brick wall on purpose and wound up in the hospital. Then he got real paranoid and told his family that I had a vendetta against him, and that I was why he was so messed up.

It was hard, because he'd been my best friend. And he was really talented. I tried my best to help him, but he built up all these imaginary things in his head about me, including that I was drugging him, which, needless to say, had no basis in fact at all. I had to stop my communication with him because it went too far. But it really broke my heart.

When the label said that they wanted to sign me, I felt like it was a product of my really attracting that energy and also being proactive about the situation, even if they didn't hit me back for a long time. Once I found those producers to make music with and was flooding them with new music all the time, they helped me a lot, too. The producers and the label all saw how hungry I was, and how I was striving to be better. And I feel like I've always gotten better with every project I drop, still to this day.

About three years after I met Kanye and his team, the contract came. It took three years of my not going to college, turning down all my scholarships, and focusing on music, reading, and building myself up.

I was embarrassed, too, that for so long it wasn't working out. It was taking years. And a lot of my friends would say, "What's going on? What's taking so long? Why aren't you on this album?" Or "You could have gone to school. At this point, I almost have a degree. You could've done the same." The girl I was dating at the time, Ashley, was so smart and so beautiful, and she was going to Michigan State. When I went up to see her, she'd bring me to her family's house and they'd ask, "What does he do?"

She'd say, "He's a rapper."

"Is he in school?"

"No," she'd say, but she confidently defended me.

I dreaded Sunday dinners because I had no updates for my grandmother. I almost enrolled in community college to get some credits. At the last minute, my mom reminded me, "Stick to it." She said that I had to remember why I was doing these things, and I had to have faith in myself. I looked down at that invisible bridge of faith, and I knew that I would get to the other side of it. I just had to keep walking. Things started eventually paying off after I put out mixtapes. I signed my record deal in 2008, and I'd met Kanye in 2005, so it took that long.

But then still, in 2008, after I signed, I was just hustling and putting out music to grow my fan base organically. Then, in 2010, I was on the cover of *XXL*'s Freshman 10 list. That's one of the most prestigious covers you could be on, because *XXL* is a staple in rap music. Every year, they do a list of the ten newcomers they think are going to be big. One of my main goals at the time was to be on the Freshman 10 list. And I finally was on it in 2010. That was the year a lot of my friends were graduating college.

But I had that honor, and after the photo shoot, I hung out with Nipsey Hussle and Wiz Khalifa and J. Cole. I looked at it as kind of my diploma. Now I was ready to go forward in the music industry. It was so gratifying. I finally had something to show for all the hard work I'd been putting in.

It wasn't until 2011 that my album came out—six whole years after I first met Kanye. There were so many ups and downs. I **trusted** in God because I did not have that much confidence in myself. I was twenty-two and winging it. I ended up having a lot of success and hit songs on the radio. And that was my cue to reaffirm my goals and start thinking bigger. Because that was originally all I'd ever imagined: a record deal, a song on the radio. The success let me **trust** myself more going forward.

But once I was on the label, I saw that even a record deal and a song on the radio don't guarantee success. There were a whole bunch of other artists signed to G.O.O.D. Music, too, and it didn't work out for a lot of them. I knew that I didn't want to fall into the same category as some of those other artists who never took off. I had to strategically figure out how I could take this co-sign that I was so grateful for and use it to my advantage—to fulfill my desires, to take care of my family, to make everyone who'd invested in me proud, including my mom and grandma. Every day, I asked myself, *How can I progress?* That is why you need to have a strategy, and you have to keep reestablishing your strategy with every new win.

When that pressure hits you and that adrenaline kicks in and the stress is on, you have to remember to have the confidence to stick to who you are, what you believe in, and the practices you've put in place for yourself—and not to compromise to match everyone else's ideas about you. It takes a lot of confidence and courage to stand firmly in your sense of self, to **trust** your talent. You have to be willing to succeed or fail by your decisions. You have to do your best on whatever road you take, without making excuses.

After my parents split up, my dad stayed in Detroit, just a few miles away. He rearranged his whole life to be around us. He wasn't there for us all the time, but I recognized even then that his making that sacrifice was big. He had no ties to Detroit, but he wanted to be in the same city as his kids, and he still resides there to this day.

In elementary and middle school, I would go to my dad's house on the weekends and play basketball with other kids on the street. He lived in a not-so-nice neighborhood, off of Linwood and Six Mile. It could get really real over there.

One of the worst times involved one of my friends over there named DeShawn. We were playing basketball one day, and he accidentally elbowed me in the face going up for a rebound and gave me a black eye. It was no big deal, but I wound up thinking a lot about that black eye because DeShawn was murdered a few days after that.

I can't remember if it was for his shoes or for his glasses. There were a lot of stories like that back then, so I mix up the facts sometimes. But I couldn't get over how I still had a black eye from him even after he was dead. That taught me about how fast life can change. Seeing tragedy come to friends like DeShawn, I felt like the stakes were incredibly high. And so I've paid a lot of attention to success stories, especially ones that take place in Detroit.

Fast-forward: Once I got to talk to music legend Berry Gordy. We were at a party celebrating the anniversary of Motown, and soon after I met him, we got to talking about what it takes to succeed.

"Man, I failed at everything in life until I was thirty-three," he said. "I failed at every single thing, man. Hundreds of things—magazines, a bunch of other projects, too. It took me all those times of failing to make something actually work for me."

In 1958, Berry Gordy founded Tamla Records, which would go on to become Motown Record Corporation. Motown wasn't an overnight success. It took years to become what it would be. When Gordy started, he couldn't even get the name he wanted for the record label (Tammy Records) because it was already taken. But he didn't let that stop him, and within three years, he had a #1 hit on his hands: "Please Mr. Postman" by the Marvelettes. Over the next decade, he signed Smokey Robinson and the Miracles, the Supremes, the Four Tops, the Jackson 5, Stevie Wonder, Marvin Gaye, and more.

How many people would've given up by the fifth, tenth, twentieth time of **trying**? So many would've said, "I'm going to go work at the factory, man. I'm done with this." Then finally he came up with the idea and had an opportunity to create Motown Records and had amazing artists. He was on fire. All those failures taught him lessons that he applied to his business.

What I heard in his story was this: You've got to keep going, because your day will come. If your heart's in the right place and your intentions are good and you keep sharpening your craft, you're doing the work, and that's all you're supposed to be doing.

Can you ask yourself, every day, what is likeliest to get you where you want to go? And then can you find a way to do that? When you're working toward your dreams, don't be scared. Don't be afraid to take your time. Don't think that your time is running out or that you have a small window of opportunity.

Your window of opportunity is open as long as you believe that it is. You are never too young, you're never too old, you're never washed up. You can always defy the odds. You can always change the game. You can always find a new way to do what you want to do. You have to believe that. Your only task is to **strategiz**e how you're going to do it and then **try** to make it happen like your life depends on it—because it very well may.

What are your short-term,
long-term, and in-between goals?

How can you be proactive so that,
once opportunity comes, you'll be ready?
Think of three steps, big or small, that
would take you to your goal and list them.
Do one thing today that will take you
in that direction.

Worrying about money is the easiest way to push it away, and a big waste of time—time you could be using to attract the money you desire. It's all energy.

CHAPTER FOUR

The Fluidity of Fortune

▪ *accepting, strategizing, trying, trusting, manifesting*

WAITING SO LONG FOR A record contract was an early lesson in how good fortune, like money, can always come and go. **Accepting** this meant unlearning some things I'd internalized about money and luck.

Growing up middle class in Detroit, we lived off credit cards for stretches of time or just got by paycheck to paycheck. In that Northlawn house, I was introduced to both the fear of losing money and the idea of scarcity, or not having enough money. I even saw my mom crying over bills. She worked two jobs and was still in debt. Sometimes we had roaches because the city was working on the sewer system. I saw my dad busting his ass, still not having enough. It was something I couldn't understand when I was young, but it imprinted on me as "How does everyone work so much and we still don't have enough money?"

There were definitely times when I didn't have enough for the things I wanted. I used to get made fun of in high school for wearing the same clothes a few times a week. There was this one guy who said, "Man, how many times you going to wear them khakis? Eight times a week?" My backpack was a mess, too. All I wanted was a regular old backpack, but I had an orthopedic bag that my mom got me to make sure I'd have good posture. It was the biggest backpack in the world. *Nerd alert.* I hated it so much.

Ultimately, I wanted to be financially free. I knew I wanted to do something where I made enough money to actually enjoy life and not work all the time. I noticed that, in the jobs my mom and my dad were working, they were never enjoying themselves. Not to say that they didn't like some aspects of their jobs or that they didn't sometimes have great days, but I could tell the work wasn't fulfilling them. I wanted to make money. I wanted to give my mom a better life, straight up. And I wanted to experience a better life for myself. But I also wanted to find a sense of purpose in how I earned my money.

When I was fifteen years old, I got my first summer job. I worked at my boy Brandon's dad's construction company, sweeping up for about a hundred dollars a week. His dad was looking out for us. I ended up buying my own clothes for school because I knew that there wouldn't be a budget for that any other way. I always knew there was an opportunity for me, especially if I could go out and earn.

As I mentioned, when I was seventeen, I worked as a telemarketer. I sold stuff over the phone, making $150 to $180 a week if I worked every day. I was doing it after school part-time, whenever I could, to fund my rap dreams. I would take my check and spend it on studio time. I was fortunate enough that my family had a house, so I didn't have to focus on contributing to rent. I was able to pour everything into recording.

The first experience I had with a real chunk of money was when I got my first record deal. It was for $15,000. I could have gotten more if I'd sold my publishing rights, but I felt like that wasn't the move.

When I got my first check from G.O.O.D. Music, signed by Donda West, Kanye's mom, I framed it.

I was happy, but at the same time, I knew that I needed to hold on to the money, and it immediately felt like water in my hands. I took my girlfriend at the time out to get some ice cream and thought, *It's already going away!*

I've since learned that money is a fluid thing. It's like blood—if you let it sit too long, it coagulates and is no good. You have to keep it flowing, and it takes money to make money. You can't be scared of losing money to gain money.

That $15,000 ended up being spent on I don't even know what. I went back to zero. I was still living at home with my mom, in the same bedroom I grew up in. I was broke again and depressed. Then I thought: *Okay, I earned this check by making music, and I can always make more music.*

I decided to **strategize**. I started listing all the ways I could make money: by putting music out and gaining more of a fan base, doing live shows. I started **trying** harder than ever.

Sometimes the shows would be for free. Sometimes I would make $250, and I put it all back into the music. The more music I put out, the more popular I became. I used G.O.O.D. Music's co-sign for promotion, and I was able to get a lot of people to tune in.

Those were the years I was straight grinding. Once some of my boys and I drove my Chevy Impala all the way from Detroit to New York City, about ten hours, for an opening spot at a club called the Knitting Factory. Kid Cudi and a few other artists were in the lineup as well, and this was early in all our careers. Detroit is the Motor City, so I wasn't fazed by it, but the intensity and aggressiveness of driving in New York was new to me. We all stayed in the same hotel room, of course. I got a bed but other people were sleeping on the floor. One guy slept in the bathtub. I might have made a few hundred bucks, but the real reward was having my first experience of performing to a packed crowd in New York.

Since then, I've had some of my greatest moments in and around that city. I did a "fan activation" in-store for adidas where we shut down a street in Soho, and I leaned out a window to see tons of fans cheering up at me. After starting out in smaller venues like S.O.B.'s, Terminal 5, and Irving Plaza, I've performed at Madison Square Garden, Radio City Music Hall, and MetLife Stadium in New Jersey, and worked my way up to the biggest stage at Summer Jam. My fan base kept growing and growing. It took a while to build it up in those early years, but as my audience grew, my show rates would grow, too. It started at $250 a show, then I got $500, then $1,500. Sometimes there would be no shows for a while, and I'd be broke again. But I would **trust** the universe, knowing that if I kept doing what I knew I was supposed to do, the universe would provide. I started to believe in myself and to **accept** these rises and falls in my fortunes. I thought, *Even if I do everything right, the money's still going to keep coming and going.*

Sometimes I talked to the universe like it was a person. I didn't demand anything. I just explained why I'd love more money—so I could have more positive experiences, so I could move to LA and be closer to the business that I was **trying** to pursue, so I could take care of my family and give some money to my mom, so I could stop spending all the money my grandma saved for me to go to college on studio sessions. My grandma saved that money for me for her whole life, after all. I told the universe I didn't want all her work and saving for me to be for nothing.

After many years of struggle, I **manifested** real abundance. I got paid half a million dollars for a single show. When I crossed the threshold of having made $1 million from my music, at twenty-four years old, I reminded myself, *Oh shit, now I got a million dollars. But like that $15,000, this could be gone at some point, too.*

The truth is, there's no one-to-one correlation between how hard someone works and how much money they have. There are billionaires out there who work an hour a day making more money than thousands of hardworking people combined. I know people who are working two shifts, eighteen-hour days, who are still struggling. I don't want to say the concept of needing to work hard for big rewards isn't true, but it doesn't always apply. Or at least it isn't that simple.

People always said that playing video games wasn't going to get you anywhere in life. Now some gamers are getting multimillion-dollar contracts. I know a streamer who gets paid $70 million for playing and giving his commentary. He is a full-fledged professional, idolized by a lot of kids.

For so long, so many people said, "Rapping's a waste. You're wasting your time doing that." But plenty of the people who had the insight to say "No, actually, this is what I'm passionate about, and I'm going to take it seriously" ultimately got rewarded one way or another. There is no such thing as a waste of time. And what are we here for if not to feel fulfilled? There is no such thing as throwing your life away on something if it makes you happy.

There is no denying that money is very important. There are also things that are important—and even invaluable—that aren't money. One of them is believing in yourself and **accepting** that pretty much whatever you do, you're going to go through ups and downs.

That's not to say don't save or invest money. I don't spend my money frivolously. There are lessons in being very wise with your money and not being excessive that I got from my family. I have a little bit of that in me, but I don't have the fear that they had. I **accept** money as a thing that I'll have or not have at various points in my life, and whether I have it or not doesn't have any bearing on my core identity or my personal value. I've done a lot of work to find and make good investments in my community: real estate, startups, Black-owned businesses that I believe in that I can feel good about supporting while also having faith that they'll help my money to grow.

I called my album *Finally Famous* because that's what we called our crew before I even got signed. I want to do my best to help other people have that feeling, that "famous" just means getting recognized at any level for your talent and "finally" because nothing happens overnight.

Worrying about money takes so much energy that could go to better things. I look back on my childhood and realize my family was stressed out about money all the time. It cost them so much joy. And their worry put no more cash into their pockets. Now I put my energy into what I can control, and I **accept** that money will come and go. I've always liked the saying "If you're chasing money, that means it's running away from you."

A lot of the things people think of as safe are not necessarily safe. I have a friend who went freelance when everyone was telling her to get a "stable" job working for a big company. Instead, she started her own company. A few years later, her company was so successful that the big company hired her company as a contractor and paid her well for her services.

A while back, I went to Uganda and saw all these people in the hood. I thought, *Man, this seems like a rough life.* But I also saw people playing soccer with each other, smiling and running in the middle of the street. There were so many things they didn't have. But you'd look in their eyes and think, *Oh, damn, they look really happy*.

At the time, I was living in a big mansion and feeling depressed, and here were people living in self-made huts, smiling. Money solves a lot of problems in people's lives, yes, but no matter what you have or don't have, you're in control of how you feel. You're in control of your emotions. That's why they're *your* emotions. How much cash you have on hand has surprisingly little to do with those feelings. Attitude matters more, no matter how much you have. I can share what helped me then and helps me now: knowing that, regardless of how much money is there, I'll always have enough love for my family and also myself.

My family would fight about money and cry about money. They'd say things like "Money doesn't grow on trees" or "We don't have money for that." Those were facts to them. But I think a lot of damage was done with those words. Knowing what I know now, I'd never tell my son, "There's no money for what you want." I might be honest that his mother and I would have to **strategize** to make something happen, and that there might need to be trade-offs or sacrifices, but I'd **try** to make it seem like anything was possible. Because everything *is* possible.

Do you have fears around money? Are they fears that you developed on your own or something your family passed on to you? What would financial freedom feel like to you? Lock onto that feeling.

I’ve rarely learned any of my lessons the easy way.

CHAPTER FIVE

When Something Needs to Change

▪ *accepting, trying, trusting, manifesting*

AS A CHILD, I ALWAYS wanted to be more and have more. Once I had everything I could have wanted as an adult, it still wasn't enough. This cycle could have continued for the rest of my life, but I'm so glad I learned a better and healthier way. I got clear about what I desired in life. I realized that whatever I achieved externally didn't necessarily help with inner peace. I'd been able to coast for a while, but when things got rough, I learned what was missing. The hard times were catalysts for doing introspective work. I've never learned any of my lessons the easy way. (One of the reasons for writing this book is to hopefully save other people from the struggles I've gone through.)

We experience things all the time that we can't see but we know are there: oxygen, love, emotion, and, most essential of all, faith. As I've said, faith is like an invisible bridge. You don't physically see how you're going to get across, but you know it's there. You step off the cliff, **trusting** that you're not going to fall, and you don't. That's what faith is.

In my song "Nothing Is Stopping You," the first lyrics are, "I know I'm gonna get it, I just don't know how." And maybe we don't need to know how. If we just **accept** that whatever's meant for us is coming our way, we don't have to necessarily worry about how it's going to happen. We just have to put our attention on the intention and ask, "What can I do to water the seed?"

Everything is made easier by coming at hardship from a place of faith—whether that be faith in a higher being, faith in the universe, or simply faith in yourself. Whenever my faith wavers, I look to other people's stories for encouragement. For example, one day Steve Harvey told a personal story on his show. He talked about a time in his life when he was broke and **trying** to make it as a stand-up comedian. He was sleeping in his car. He had $35 to his name. Then he was asked to appear at the Apollo in New York City, but he couldn't afford the trip.

Someone ended up booking him in Orlando two days before the show in New York for $150. He was able to get to Orlando, and then he called the Apollo and said, "Hey, can I still open up?"

The guy said, "Actually, you still can."

He somehow made it there, and because he didn't have anywhere to stay, he asked if he could stay in a dressing room. They said, "That's weird, but sure. You could stay in a dressing room all day."

Jamie Foxx was there, all these other people, too, and all the other performers got booed and bombed. Everyone said, "Man, that crowd is tough." But Steve went out there and tore it down. It changed his whole life. They booked him again. His name started buzzing off of these shows.

An incredible story, start to finish, and one that highlights those moments when you can feel your destiny coming for you. Just submit and let it happen. That's a feeling that money can't buy—that's inspiration. At the end of telling this story, Steve Harvey said, "There's one guarantee: if you give up, it will never happen. Faith is everything, God is always on time. He's never too late."

Whether you like to talk about things in terms of God or not, the point is the same: get clear about what you desire in life—which often comes from **trying** new things and letting yourself dream—and you can achieve anything.

The quickest way to believe something is to keep repeating it and to keep living in it, because your subconscious will believe it before your conscious self does. And if you believe in that, if you believe in the power of **manifesting**, the power of saying things out loud and letting them come to you, then you will get your shot and your opportunity in whatever it is you're doing, especially if you're righteous with it, especially if you have good intentions.

SEAN'S SAMPLE MANIFESTATIONS

Here are just a few examples:

1. Writing this book. This is something I have always desired, but for years I never really took the time to ask, *Man, how can I make this happen?* When I finally did, I was able to **manifest** the right team, the right people; they magnetized to me and helped make it happen.

2. When I was twenty-two, I put a white Mercedes-Benz on my vision board. I thought that was the ultimate level of luxury. Eventually,

I did enough shows that I could afford it. I got a white S-550 with cream leather seats and wood grain. It was smooth, so fly, and so big that I felt like I was the pastor pulling into church. The magic of material things wears off eventually, but to me that car represented my ability to achieve my goals. It was huge for me.

3. I had always desired a Jesus Piece from Jacob the Jeweler. It was such an iconic rap chain and the symbol for G.O.O.D. Music. One day, Kanye's road manager, Don C, gave me one, compliments of Ye. He gave it to me just as I was leaving LA for Detroit, and I took it out on the flight. I was sitting in a middle seat in coach, and I just stared at that expensive chain, looking around, wondering if anyone could see what it was I had. It was so beautiful. And it was so much more than a chain. To me, it represented the forward momentum that I had been working so hard for.

4. One of my biggest goals growing up was to have a song on the radio. I'll never forget hearing the first actual hit I had on the radio, how much it meant to me and how cool it was. It was a song called "My Last," featuring Chris Brown. That transitioned me from a mixtape artist to someone much bigger. It was my first record to go gold. We threw a big dinner to celebrate. Now that I get gold and platinum records regularly, I probably don't appreciate it enough. I'd like to get back to celebrating it more. Every time is a gift.

5. Buying a house for my mom and grandma in the suburbs of Detroit, beginning to give back to them after all they'd given me, was a great moment. Just to be able to provide for the people I love

and the people who had already given me so much, especially in pursuit of my dreams.

6. My relationship with Noah has been the best **manifestation** of my life. When he was born, I watched him breathing while they dried him off, and I couldn't believe it. He adjusted to the world like a champ. I cut the umbilical cord and filmed it on my phone because I never wanted to forget the feeling. I look at it pretty often. And as powerful as that moment was, my bond with him has kept getting deeper and deeper. You think you've reached the limit of how much love you can feel for something that you created, and then your love goes deeper still.

A couple of years ago, I said to myself, *I'm going to focus on being creative.* Even though my accountant was a little nervous to hear I wasn't going to be working for a while, I had faith. I believed that I'd laid enough groundwork that the money would come from somewhere. It's important to stay passionate and to figure out what it is that inspires you, what makes you happy. And so, for a few months, I focused on my work, stayed open—and, as I'd hoped, the universe provided. I got a call: "How about a residency in Vegas where you go once a month?" That was something that would let me keep doing my creative work most of the time but still support myself.

Of course, even when I was doing what I was supposed to be doing, focusing on myself, I would go through ups and downs and even get depressed sometimes. Things wouldn't always go my way because I had expectations about what I was supposed to be doing. But then I would have to go back and say to myself, *Nothing is permanent, not the good or the bad. And wherever I am, I'm still going to have the opportunity to restructure, regroup, attract the necessary people in my life to help make things happen.*

When things don't go the way we want or plan, we might be tempted to stop believing. But faith is knowing that the universe could have something different or bigger planned for us than what we can imagine now.

Besides, if everything went exactly the way you wanted, how would you ever grow? How boring would life be if you knew exactly what was coming next? You'd never experience the magic of the unknown or the unexpected. That's why it's important to have faith and not be afraid to take risks.

We can't allow ourselves to be discouraged if things don't work out the way we wanted them to, because we don't know what's around the corner. When Berry Gordy didn't have success overnight, he kept going, because he knew that, with each step, he was closer to success than he was when he'd started. And it was worth it.

For me, I began to visualize that G.O.O.D. Music would reach out to me again and I would move ahead in my career. I knew it was going to happen. I had to listen to the voice inside me, listen to God telling me it would work out, and **trust** that I would be supported by faith and not fail, even if I couldn't see the next step in front of me. When I got signed as a result of that day at the radio station, that was the confirmation I needed to know that the **trust** I'd put in the universe by pursuing a career in music hadn't been wasted and I was on the path to achieving my dreams.

If you're getting a feeling of happiness researching the work you think you want to do, if you're nerding out over something, if it sparks your interest, then you're on the right track. There may be times when you hit a dead end or things may not work out the way you want them to, and it gets frustrating.

If you're **trying** to **strategize** and you don't know what you're doing or feel like you've hit a wall, that's when you need to start looking at people who've done what you're **trying** to do. Read their books. Listen to them talk about their path. What have they done that you can incorporate into your own life? Are there lessons for you there? Make a list of all the things you want to accomplish and break them down into steps. Can you do the first step toward your dream? And then another step? And if you don't know what you want to accomplish, just focus on being happy. Usually when you're operating from a place of happiness, things tend to happen in your favor.

Appreciating where you're at, knowing things will change, and being willing to do anything to make things change is the recipe for welcoming more good things into your life. Desires motivate you, but you can't let them consume you. You can only control yourself—how you approach the work, the attitude you bring to it, and how hard you apply yourself. When you bring those things into alignment with who you are and where you're heading, eventually good things start to happen.

What do you want? What do you need? What's within your control? What changes would help you get there? Visualize getting what you want, and lock onto that feeling.

Gratitude is a magnet for more of what you're thankful for. . . . Duh.

CHAPTER SIX
Gratitude

▪ *accepting*

SOMETIMES WE'RE SO CAUGHT UP in our own lives and our own storylines and our own drama and trauma that we miss or don't acknowledge our blessings. But that acknowledgment will change your whole experience and your whole vibration. It might take a tragedy to force us to **accept** that we are all part of one greater movement; otherwise, we can fail to truly see what's in front of us. In this way, even the worst times can give us something important.

In *The Seven Spiritual Laws of Success*, Deepak Chopra says, "As long as you're giving, you will be receiving." He says you should never show up to someone's house empty-handed—that it's enough to bring a flower, a card that says something about the person you're visiting, a compliment, or a prayer. You wish them the best possible life that they can have, and doing that lifts up your vibration, too.

It is so important to practice gratitude in your everyday life. Find magic in the simple things that people can take for granted. Take breathing, for example. Imagine if you struggled every time you took a breath. You have to look for your blessings and then really appreciate them.

We need to allow not only the big things to motivate us but also the little things. They build up to your bigger success. With every step you take, you evolve. Let's remember to take the small wins. Whatever you intend for that day, even if it's just taking a shower, you need to celebrate it. That will give confirmation to the world that you appreciate the gain and you're ready for more. Gratitude acts like a magnet for more of what you're thankful for. I tell myself every day: Remember to be grateful. Remember to be joyful.

A lot of us get caught up in counting material things as blessings, and they are, but a far greater gift is the ability to live another day. If you truly feel that, you'll know what it's like to be rich. And do you have other things to be thankful for? Do you have your health? Do you have a good friend? Do you have a special talent? Do you enjoy a cup of coffee in the morning or a beautiful sunset in the evening?

When I was little, one of my teachers developed cancer and lost the glands in her mouth that produced saliva. As I remember it, she had to sip water almost constantly to make speaking bearable, but she never stopped teaching. For the first time in my life, I felt thankful for my saliva. Who is thankful for their spit? This taught me from an early age to be grateful for my body. Knowing how fast time passes and how we can't take our physical being for granted is one of the things that has taught me to be present in every moment.

There is always time to make your life everything you ever dreamed of and more. When you do, you're opening up space for what else the universe might have for you. It might be a new passion; it might be a new idea. You never know. I expect to keep learning about myself, other people, and our divine nature for as long as I live. It's a never-ending journey.

You have to recognize the beauty of life—the pleasure you feel when the warmth of the sun hits your face and you take the time to breathe in. That's when you are your optimal "you."

What are you grateful for?
How do you express that gratitude?
Is there a way for you to receive
more of the things you're grateful
for in your life? If so, what is it?

The times my faith was tested, I either made it through it or made it to it, but it never failed. It showed me what I was made of.

CHAPTER SEVEN
Full Faith

▪ *accepting, strategizing, trying, trusting, manifesting*

ON "BOUNCE BACK," I SAY, "With the faith of a mustard seed, I kept growing / I knew that this life was meant for me." On the cover of the album is a picture of me at two different ages, separated by a tree. I made sure there was a tree at the listening parties to represent the idea of growth through faith. Honestly, all we have to do to witness a miracle is to walk outside and realize how the sun, gravity, and everything is in perfect synchronicity to let us live comfortably on this planet.

I surround myself with reminders that the times my faith has been tested are also the times when I needed faith the most. One example is when my third album came out. My first album did well. My second one didn't sell as many copies. So my third one was poised to be a defining moment in my career. A lot of people had lost faith in me. Not the people closest to me, but people on the fringes of my life. They said, "Oh, he's done, an in-and-out type of guy career-wise." I would hear a lot of chatter of that type through the grapevine.

While I was waiting for the album to come out, I felt called to make a freestyle as a surprise for my fans. I took an impromptu trip to the studio and stayed in there all night and recorded this freestyle that I ended up putting out on SoundCloud. Soon after, I had a wild forty-eight hours of press in New York. After this whirlwind, I finally got about half an hour by myself in the hotel room. I spent those thirty minutes praying and taking time alone. All of a sudden, it was two minutes before the album was going to come out. In that final moment, I started praying to my grandma, who had passed away a few months before that.

Even though I couldn't hear my grandma or see her, I felt her energy. It was one of the times in my life when I said, "Man, am I tripping right now?" And I replied to myself, "No, you have to have faith that what you believe is real, and that's it. If you believe it, it's real."

So I kept praying and **trusting** the universe and God. I thought, *If this is meant to be, this will work out. This will be my first number one album*. I was going over all these things in my head, and all I kept hearing was, "Have faith in it."

I took that as my grandma telling me that. I felt her energy there with me in the room.

After the album dropped, there was quiet for about ten minutes, and then my phone started blowing up. People said, "Congrats, it's amazing! It's a hit!"

You don't find out if an album goes number one until a few days after it comes out, but I was getting word that it was clearly going to go number one because it was so successful so fast. My label hit me up and said, "Wow, congrats, man! You're going to have your first number one album!"

It was major. It was incredible. It changed my life, honestly. Everything came together: I'd **accepted** the goodness of what I'd made. I **strategized** the best way to get it out into the world. I **tried** my best to share what I had. I **trusted** that the universe would provide, and then I **manifested** the best possible outcome.

I walked out of my hotel room to go to a release party, and it was great. From there, I was doing radio promo in other cities. At 2:00 a.m., we flew to Atlanta to do the morning show there. I didn't sleep because on the plane I had a writer from *Complex* magazine interviewing me. I was running on caffeine.

Before flying back to LA, we stopped in Detroit for the night, and I did a performance at the legendary St. Andrew's. That's where Eminem used to battle-rap, and a lot of scenes from *8 Mile* took place there. It's a smaller venue, real intimate, but it was a classic, and I did an impromptu performance, and my family was there with me—my brother, my mom, my dad. We celebrated with Detroit-style pizza from one of my favorite places, Jet's, and even though I was so exhausted, I had the best time. Those good times become more possible when you **trust** your heart and let out what you have to share with the world.

What do you have to
share with the world?

What's holding you
back from sharing it?

List five miracles in your life.
Give thanks for them.
This is a sure way over time
to strengthen your faith.

The number one scorer of all time in the NBA is also the player with the most missed shots. It's a part of life.

CHAPTER EIGHT
Hitting a Wall

▪ *accepting, strategizing, trying, trusting, manifesting*

THE MOST DEPRESSED I EVER got was in 2017. Until then, the worst period was when I got signed and then nothing happened for more than a year. But this time, everything was happening for me, so I found it incredibly confusing that I was so unhappy.

I was rich and famous. My career was going great, and I was on tour. I had everything I'd ever wanted. At age eleven, I'd said, "I'm gonna be a rapper someday." And here I was, doing it at the highest level! But nothing ever felt like enough.

And this time around, I had two new problems: I was working all the time, with no balance that allowed space for a personal life. And in the process of being so overworked, I'd become super-addicted to Adderall.

I was on tour with Rihanna in 2016 and sleeping poorly, so every time I got onto the bus, which had a studio in it, I would fall asleep. I was so tired of not being able to record. I had a studio bus; I needed to use it! A DJ friend said, "Yo, man, you take this, and you can stay awake."

"I don't fuck wit drugs," I said.

"No, bro, it's not a drug like that," he said. "Students take it! It's like vitamins."

I'm a smart man, but I wanted to believe him. So I tried it. The first time I took it, I got so much done. But I felt so sick afterward.

My security guard said, "Man, you need to drink water while you're doing it," so I was drinking a lot of water, and it helped balance out the Adderall some, but I knew I was doing damage to my mind and body. I was also abusing my body in other ways, eating trash food all the time, staying up super late. Most people who are prescribed Adderall need it. I wasn't prescribed it, and I didn't actually benefit from it in the long run. I'm not hyperactive. I can focus. Later, a doctor told me I'd strained my cardiovascular system by taking Adderall.

When I was on that tour, I wasn't inspired, and this was a time when I needed to be inspired. When you do Adderall, it makes you feel like you're wide-awake and focusing. It let me feel like I was actually accomplishing something, when the core creativity I needed to make the music that I wanted to make wasn't in me at that moment. I was forcing it.

After my next album came out, in 2017, I started to realize that the way I was living was tearing my body up. When I would use the bathroom, it would smell like a dead body had come out of me; it was terrible. My skin was drying out. My mom has eczema, and I grew up with eczema, too, but this was a whole other level of bad skin. I was suddenly looking way older. And I was so irritable. I didn't want to talk to anyone. Without the drug, I found it hard to even get out of bed and get on with my day. The drug had given me artificial energy and happiness. When you stop a drug like that, you wind up in a state of heaviness, tiredness, and physical depletion. The thoughts that infiltrate your mind in that state can be venomous.

Not only can using these drugs get you addicted but they can cause major damage over time, including heart problems and depression. I didn't take it for that long—only about a year. But it was enough. Once I started to feel like I couldn't do what I was doing without Adderall, that's when I knew I had a problem. That's when I knew I'd fucked up. What I needed was to get off it and heal.

I quit Adderall cold turkey. Then I got depressed and confused, and even suicidal. I felt so awful, even though I was living in a so-called dream house. My career was going fine; there were ups and downs, but nothing so severe that I felt like I couldn't handle it. Little things became too much for me to handle—a stressful phone call, posting a photo online. I didn't want to talk to anyone. I fell out with my mom. I felt unworthy. My friends would call me to go out, but I'd say no because I didn't feel like I deserved to have a good time. It kept getting worse and worse and worse. I was pissed off, mad at everyone.

I didn't realize the relationship between the drug and my brain, how much I wasn't able to feel happiness naturally anymore.

I'd been focusing on work to the detriment of everything else. When you're starting out in a field like music, you feel that you have to be fully focused. You come to believe that you've got to keep your foot on the gas, and you've got to keep going. You're not secure in yourself. You still have to work to believe that you were meant to be there.

I didn't have someone to tell me, "You deserve peace. You can take time out and live your life, and the work will still be there. In fact, you can probably get more done if you pace yourself. You have to refill your well."

When your brain gets altered by something that feeds the cycle you're stuck in, you may find it even harder to believe in yourself.

A lot of people depend on drugs to feel good about themselves, at least for a little while. But drugs are a synthetic high. When the drugs wear off, they actually leave you feeling lower. Now I'm in a new place. I haven't had a drink since 2021, and I don't do drugs. I'm grateful to have been given the grace to work all of that out. Remember, for people who are depressed: alcohol is a depressant, and antidepressants don't balance that out. The more you get attached to alcohol, the more you're digging a hole that you'll have to climb out of.

Over time, I turned my habits around and started taking better care of myself. I started taking minerals, vitamins, and other supplements, and I've also stayed disciplined. I started working out, and I became stronger. And what I've found is that the real high comes when you tap into a natural euphoria, whether it's a passion you have or an environment that makes you feel alive—nature, Grandma's house, a concert.

When you find what feeds you, it's essential to carve out time to do those things, to experience what gives you joy. Discovering a passion, taking yourself seriously, and working on yourself through the lens of whatever that passion is—those are the steps that lead you to truly realize the highs of self-love.

My song "High" is about the temporary highs you can find, but truly going "higher" is about the high you get from within yourself. You go higher when you start doing the real work. Expanding your mind, forming new behavioral patterns, practicing self-love and forgiveness—all these things serve your greater good. And if everyone practiced them, think about how much better off the world would be.

Going higher isn't about achieving more success. It's about becoming your best self—a person who's at peace, who feels happiness, who has meaningful relationships, and who is achieving personal, professional, and creative goals. Thinking about these things is the key to everything. It's about understanding who you are and what your purpose is. It's about deciding where you want to go and then going there.

I don't want to make too much of my bad experience with prescription drugs. They save lives all the time and are necessary for many people to face the day or get things done. And I've seen recreational drugs help some people reach new levels of creativity, too. I love the Beatles. I don't know what life would've been like if they'd never experimented with drugs. But drugs aren't for me.

When you go off Adderall, you crash. I learned so many lessons during the years I spent getting off it, perhaps most importantly that I have to give myself over to God's time instead of measuring everything against a calendar.

When you become dependent on a substance like that, you feel like you've lost yourself. That was hard for me to deal with and get through. But like the first time I hit bottom, I started working on myself again. I realized that I'd begun the work on my spiritual life as a teenager, but I hadn't kept it up. I almost thought success would substitute for spiritual growth, but it did the opposite and knocked me off my path. It was only when I started reading again, finding people who could help me, that things got better. I reclaimed my motivation to spiritually connect with myself. And this time I dug deeper.

It took a while before I found my creativity again. I felt burned out. I'd always loved to rap, but I thought seriously about giving it up. Everything was just so hard. Looking back at the projects I did put out at that time, I can see now that they weren't inspired. I was listening to a lot of people around me. They meant well, but when you're an artist and your name is on it, it has to be your soul going into the work. It got to where I trusted other people more than I trusted myself. And I gave them more than I gave myself—my time, my energy, my happiness. I got burned out to the point where I became checked out.

In the studio, days would go by without my having a single idea. I thought to myself: *Either this wall's going to fall on me, or I need to find a way to climb over it.*

No one thought it was a good idea to take time off. "You have responsibilities!" they said. "You have endorsement deals! Contracts!"

But I just couldn't do it. I was breaking down. My therapist asked me one time, "What makes you happy?"

I couldn't even answer the question. I started crying because I had no idea what made me happy anymore. I was doing what I had to do: work, press, charity. I was fulfilling my obligations to my family. But I had no time to recharge.

I started **trying** all kinds of things to see if any filled that hole. One was to learn to shoot, but I went to a gun range and wasn't that into it at the time. Another was skydiving. When I first jumped out of the plane I thought, *Well, that was a terrible idea*. But a few seconds into it, I felt exhilarated. No need to do it again anytime soon.

I tried having it out with the people around me. I've got a great relationship with my mom, but one day I went off on her and said I didn't want her to be a part of my life anymore. She didn't deserve that. No one I yelled at in those days did.

It just took time alone, taking care of myself, to start to heal and to remember who I was and what I wanted. Once I took the pressure off myself, I started having fun again. That's when the passion came back. And when it did, I made it really clear to the people around me that if my name was on something, I had to believe in it completely. That was a big lesson I learned during that time: if you're not feeling it, you shouldn't be doing it. I had to learn how to say no to things, even some very cool things, if they didn't feel right for me. I had to **try** new things. And I had to get okay with having dry spells.

Ultimately, I've made peace with the music I released during that time, and with having lost myself for a while. There's no guide on how to be human. I forgave myself, and I'm glad for the lessons I learned from it. One of the greatest lessons was that I need to focus on why I'm doing things, not just on what I'm doing. My number one goal is to inspire. I'll do that by making music or by any medium available to me. If someone's saying "You gotta do something now! You gotta stay hot!" that can be bad advice. Because I don't want to be chasing some kind of superficial success of the moment. I'm doing my best to lift people up and motivate them.

In the end, because of how things had gotten with my Adderall addiction and all the work I had to do to get healthy again, I bowed out of the game for three years. That was time spent getting better, in both body and mind. I started applying intentions to my life that have changed its trajectory forever. Whatever you go through, it's always a blessing somehow. Tough times build our character. They made me stronger. I learned so much about myself and about why I do what I do.

Now, knowing that I've come out on the other side, I feel like rock bottom isn't even an option for me anymore. With all these tools available, none of us should ever need to go that low. If we're on our way to rock bottom, we should be able to speak up—even if only to ourselves—and say, "Hey, I'm about to hit a low point. I need to regroup, reorganize, take some time, and figure some things out right now."

No matter what happens with me, if nothing works out ever again in my career, I don't think I could ever be as depressed as I was back then. But I did the work to have a stronger foundation for the next rough patch.

To be a human who is fully present in the world is a lot. We're forever changing, and we have to constantly rediscover ourselves. To live a rich life, we need to keep learning and growing forever until we're gone. No matter how old you are, you will still have to start over again all the time. My hope is that some of these tools will be as helpful to you as they were to me.

My family has battled with depression in ways I'm only beginning to understand now. My dad is one of the happiest, coolest people to be around, and I recently learned that even he has struggled with thoughts of suicide.

When I asked him about it, he said, "Man, at seventy-something years old, I just feel like I want my life to be a certain way, and it's not that way. I'm striving, and I'm working toward it, but, man, I just feel sometimes like I've lived long enough."

"Well, how would you feel if I talked like that?" I said to him. "How would you feel if I said I wanted to take my life?"

"Oh, man," he said, "I would rather jump off a bridge ten times than you ever do it."

I reminded him that we've got to remember that we're here for a reason, even if sometimes we can't quite tell what that reason is. You are unique, but you're not alone.

And yet I understood what he was saying. I've been suicidal before, too. I've dealt with depression and anxiety. My depression was intense, and I felt totally alone in it, like I was by myself on an island. That was such a dark time in my life. I felt like I was being tested. Writing "Deep Reverence" helped me to make sense of it, and also to turn that testing into testimony.

It was only by going deep into nurturing myself that I was able to get better. That's when I really expanded my meditations and dove into books, really took time away from music and put time in on myself. But I'm happy I experienced that, because I wouldn't be who I am without it. Those are the makings of a human being. I wear those hard times like badges of honor.

If you're having a hard time, you don't have to be ashamed, and you don't have to hide it. You can tell people, like I have. Not only does it free you from shame but it also gives your suffering meaning. It lets the next person realize they're not alone. Plus, when you come out on the other side, then you're actually in the light, and you set an example for others to make the same journey.

I still get overwhelmed sometimes, especially when I'm tired. I have depressing thoughts. The difference is that now I know how to combat them, so they don't last. That's the beauty and the promise of working on yourself. It doesn't mean you're happy every second, but you have the tools to get better faster.

Sometimes we let our moods determine how our day goes, but we can choose not to let our moods run the show. There's a difference between being mad and recognizing the feeling but deciding not to let it take us over. Now when I feel myself getting upset over something, I say, "Let me chill out and revisit this when I'm not so in my feelings." That can make all the difference.

When we embrace the five practices—**accept**, **strategize**, **try**, **trust**, and **manifest**—we gain the capacity to change things. We have to use our power productively and with focus. You can't expect something good to come to you by holding on to the past. Only by moving forward with a clear heart will you reach your full potential.

People sometimes wait until they're at their most desperate to decide that something needs to change, that they need to start praying, meditating, and doing work on themselves to get to that higher level. This is what happened to me. I realized I needed to change, and quickly. But once I had recovered, I also knew I needed to continue to do the work, even after I had come back to "normal." Just because I'd found peace once didn't mean I'd found it for good. I've had to keep doing the work on myself to keep myself in a good mental place.

If I had begun that work at a higher level rather than waiting until I was at the bottom, maybe I could have gone to even greater heights. The goal isn't to go back to who you were before the trauma; that person doesn't exist anymore. The goal is to make space for the even better person you're becoming.

If you're in crisis, please call, text, or chat with the Suicide and Crisis Lifeline at 988, or contact the Crisis Text Line by texting TALK to 741741.

What walls have you hit in your life? How did you handle them? What did they teach you? What would you do differently now? If you knew you were going to hit another wall, what would you do to prepare? What makes you happy?

Communication is the bridge to salvation that God is holding our hands to walk across, but to make it to the other side of that bridge, you must take every step.

CHAPTER NINE

Affirmations and Agreements

accepting, strategizing, trying, trusting, manifesting

EVERY TIME I STEP INTO that booth, I have to feel like I'm the very best at what I do. If you go to work feeling like you're not the best at some aspect of it, then how are you going to have the motivation to keep going? If you're only doing something for the paycheck, it's hard to keep focused and keep pushing. If you do that long enough, it can even become torturous. But if you're looking straight at your goal, at the finish line, and not looking at people on the sidelines, then you're running your race a whole lot faster. It took me a long time to get my full confidence together, but I have it now.

Two things that have helped me so much with that focus and confidence are agreements and affirmations. They're similar, and each has an important place in my life. But they're slightly different forms of self-encouragement, at least in how I use them.

Agreements

- I will always have way more than enough money, and also opportunities that bring me wealth, abundance, financial freedom and will never need for money or financial support due to how much is easily and consistently flowing in to pursue my passions and purposes to the fullest and help uplift and inspire The Whole World and more.
- I am Operating on Devine timing in every aspect of my life and more knowing God and The Universe are fully backing me and supporting a timeline that is aligned with my personal desired timing and when things don't happen exactly when I desire them to, they happen at an even better time that always supports my life, happiness, success, passion and Joy.
- I am Happy to do my best, and be my best as a father to my son Noah and always be there when he would like mostly, but always when he needs and I am grateful to be his father and more.

Sean Anderson

IT IS DONE!!!

None of this should feel foreign, because a lot of us already make New Year's resolutions. I make them, too. Each New Year, I've always tried to pick up something new. The year 2023 was the year to focus on being a father. The year before was learning the piano. The year before, I took vocal lessons, making my voice stronger. The year before that was to make working out a part of my routine. The year before that was putting myself first. This year will be writing a book so I can share what I've learned about how to improve my mental health in case it might help other people—so if you're reading this now, it worked!

Agreements are a bit like New Year's resolutions, but you do them year-round, and they evolve as your situation changes. Maybe think of them as intentions.

One agreement that I've made with the universe recently: *God is supporting me always. Anything that happens to me is for the betterment of myself and for the greater good.*

Another: *I'm grateful that the universe will always supply me with more than I need when it comes to opportunities and inspiration.*

I have some goals that are achievable in the next year and others that are more of a reach or that stretch out into the future. I like to keep the door open in case the universe surprises me with gifts I didn't plan for.

One agreement I made when my fifth album came out was to make $2 million from merchandise for the release. We ended up making $2 million in merch in less than a month. Now I always add "and more" because I want to give the universe room to supply me with what I need *and more*. Anything I ever have an idea for, I always say

- I am Happy
- I am Inspired
- I am Grateful
- I am Confident
- I am Healthy
- I am Unstoppable
- I am Free
- I am Expanding
- I am Happy I am Noah's Dad and more.
- I am Thankful for every aspect and experience today will bring me and more.
- I am Rich in love, joy, health, money, family and more.
- I am The Best me in every way and show that in all my actions and more.
- I am supported by God and the whole Universe fully and more.
- I am attracting all the right people and experiences are desired and meant for me and more.
- I am Happy to work out for atleast an hour and

have a great leg day and more.

- I am Happy to finish all the new music I have been working on easilly and effortlessly and more.
- I am Dominating every moment of my day and more

Sean Anderson

IT IS DONE!!!

"and more," because sometimes when we get too specific, we close off the opportunities that are meant for us.

Another agreement: "I would love to have a number one bestselling book—and more." I'm going to let the universe figure out the details. Do I want it to reach a hundred thousand people? A million people?

Affirmations are more like daily pep talks: *I am brilliant. I am free. I am loving. I am unstoppable. I am confident.* One of my go-tos is *I am happy to have the protection of the universe, to be protected by the power of love.*

Affirmations are something that I say to the universe daily as a way to connect my conscious mind and my soul. I state my gratitude for what I have or say something as a way to come to believe and **accept** it, or as a way to make it so. In my experience, when you let the universe know what you're grateful for and what you want to be true, those things tend to become more present in your life. A lot of people expect good things to happen, but they never communicate that desire to the universe. Your relationship with the universe requires clear communication, just like a romantic or business relationship.

While I'm doing affirmations, I add some specifics: I'm happy to be able to put new music out into the world today to inspire people. I also like to throw in some gratitude: I'm thankful for this beautiful day we're experiencing. I'm so grateful that the sun is out and shining on us. I incorporate whatever is currently going on in my life and around me. I'm so thankful that my mother takes such good care of us. I'm so thankful for my family. Sometimes I'll go on for a couple of minutes.

And then, at the end, I'll say, "Sean Anderson." I think I came up with doing it that way because to me it sounded like signing a contract with God or the universe, making it official. I make it a declaration, almost like a demand, calling on the power God has bestowed on us. And then I take a deep breath in and a deep breath out. Once you're in a place of generosity and receptivity, it's time to talk to the universe.

Affirmations and agreements are just another way of **strategizing**, and that's something that I've been doing since I was little. I assess my situation, whatever it is, and position myself for what's going to come next. To go to the next place, you have to **strategize**. You can't sit still and expect your life to change. And the very first part of any strategy is being ready and putting yourself into the right position for good fortune to come your way.

Each day I go into a studio, I **strategize**: "What can I do to be the most productive? How can I take the most advantage of this situation for myself while benefiting everyone around me?"

The answer is to go in there and absolutely kill it, to do my very best. And to pay attention. Be a sponge.

If we're recording Monday and Friday, I build up to those days and **try** to make sure my verse is right, or I go back in on my verse and edit it. I **strategize** to impress everyone around me, because when you impress people with whatever you're doing, they take you more and more seriously. When you show your God-given talent, it counts for a lot, but what counts for way more is when they see your talent combined with your hunger and your dedication. The more prepared you are, the more you gain the respect of the people around you.

That is where I've seen so many talented people fall through the cracks. People get lazy. They don't have the discipline. Everyone has dreams. Some people have talent. But many fewer have the discipline to see it all the way through.

In my personal life, too, I make myself available for the people I care about. I work hard to make how I spend my days line up with my values. I care about my family and my music, so that's what I'm going to spend most of my day on.

I've never lacked the discipline to go higher. But sometimes it takes me a while. For instance, I kept getting started with a workout routine, and I would fall off every time. Then, in 2019, I said, "No, I'm going to stay on it. I know how important this is for my mind, body, and spirit." Since then, I've stayed on it, and I'm in the best shape of my life now. When I go to the gym, I do a full workout of my upper body, and I never skip my legs.

Of course, there are barriers, especially when I'm working a lot and am tired. But I remind myself how good I'll feel after I exercise. I put myself on a strict schedule until it became a habit, and I had other people help me with accountability, but that alone wasn't enough to keep me on track.

For so long, I'd said I wanted to work out, but whenever I tried it, I completely fell off the regimen. The only way to stick to a workout routine is to agree that your life depends on it. You have to say that this is something that you cannot live without. You have to recognize how high the stakes are, because it's not easy, and it gets frustrating. It'll wipe your energy out sometimes, especially when you have other things to do and it can't be your top priority. You have a life outside of working out, but you also have to realize how important it is and how much it helps you.

As a person who has been working out for the past five years straight, I've learned that it gives you time to focus on you, to nurture the body that you demand so much from every single day. We demand our body to wake up, to be healthy, to fight off viruses and colds, to perform, to walk, and to pick things up and carry them. I honestly feel like the least we can do is pour that energy back into our bodies, even if it's just a couple of times a week, even if it's just for twenty minutes.

It's not selfish; it's self-care. Don't ever feel guilty about taking time to build yourself up because you want to present your best self to people and put your best foot forward. Now, when it comes to the specifics of working out, everyone has a different body type. Everyone has a different regimen. Everyone isn't made to throw big weights around or to do three or four miles on a treadmill every time they work out. You have to find what works for you, and that only comes with time and experience.

For me, I have to make the decision that I want to feel and look my best. I want to take time to turn my phone off and focus on me for a little bit. Working out is probably one of the most productive things I do with my life. And that only came when I made the decision that there was no other option.

I remind myself that doing things that are good for me gives energy rather than takes it away, and that keeps me from falling out of the habit of working out. It helps so much being able to see results, too. In the past couple of years, I've put on forty pounds of muscle. And I don't know if I'd have stuck to all those good habits without reminding myself and promising myself through my affirmations and agreements.

I find that this also helps me believe in a benevolent universe. If you're not in the right headspace, you can always find evidence to support the idea that the world is against you. We all can. But, just as easily, you can find proof to back up the idea that the world is assisting you. It's a matter of where you want to put your energy. I believe there's so much value in explicitly setting those intentions and in imagining the universe as benevolent. You can do both things: ask for something, and say you're open to the universe giving you something different that you didn't know you needed.

I know the power of my subconscious. To me, the ways you perceive things and attract things dictate your whole experience in this world. I feel like it's all about the relationship between you and the universe. Speaking in positive ways about yourself and your life can trick your subconscious. When your subconscious hears "I am strong," your subconscious believes it. Your conscious mind might offer some counterarguments, but your subconscious will listen with an open heart to these messages.

I also believe in creating vision boards to make your goals tangible. Right now, I have a vision board that a spiritual teacher from Belgium named Marie Diamond created, with various colors and directions. For the "health" direction and color, I use my weight and the amount I want to lift. For the "wisdom" section, you could use Buddha or Jesus or an image of yourself meditating. I might use a picture of Noah to symbolize the wisdom I gain interacting with him.

The first vision board I ever made was a white poster board with gold foil that I felt activated it. I got out a glue stick and a stack of magazines. On it I put a white Benz, a new house, a lot of money, platinum records, a picture that looked like the relationship I wanted, accolades, crowds at the biggest festivals. I had the Coachella logo on there.

All those things came to pass. It kept piling up. I appreciated every single one.

When Coachella happened, I met with the head of the festival and played him my new album.

"Sorry it took so long to book you," he said.

I said, "It's the right time now."

When you approach it in the right way, I guarantee the universe will listen and you'll **manifest** your vision for the future.

Make three agreements with the universe. Write them down and sign your name underneath, with the words "so be it."

Repeat three affirmations three times every day for a week.

How did it make you feel?

Pressure is something I've grown to have a great relationship with. It pushes me to limits I couldn't get to by staying comfortable.

CHAPTER TEN
Therapy

▪ *trying*

THERAPY IS SUCH A GIFT for people who have extra stress that they're carrying around. They may have had traumatic experiences, but they can also have a feeling of heaviness that they can't explain. Sitting with a therapist can give you a safe place to explore your thoughts and feelings and to learn more about yourself from someone who's trained to help you explore your situation in a constructive and nurturing way. And I've found that, even if the therapist doesn't teach you anything you don't already know, taking the time out to really focus on yourself is still more than worth it. You're being intentional.

I saw my brother and my mom do counseling, so I never personally had the resistance to it that so many other people I grew up around did. But isn't it strange that the people who need help most—kids who saw a lot of terrible things when they were young, who lost their friends early, whose parents passed on trauma through their DNA—are the ones who think therapy doesn't apply to them or who want it but can't afford it?

My dad was beaten by his stepfather when he was young, and he had a stutter that he got teased for mercilessly. He grew up in Monroe, Louisiana, which was racist as shit back then. If you got caught on the wrong side of the tracks, then you'd get beaten up pretty badly. He didn't think he needed therapy until I went to therapy. Then he finally said, "Man, maybe I should **try** it." He was an instant convert. He told me, "This was awesome—just what I needed!"

Another benefit of working on yourself is that it rubs off on the people around you, your family members, and your friends. They start to think, "Well, maybe at least it wouldn't hurt to **try** to take care of myself, too. Let me **try** it."

I'm fortunate that I never was abused as a child, and I've never had a gun pulled on me directly, though I've been in the midst of a lot of guns and seen a lot of things growing up in Detroit. When I was about fifteen, I saw a person being pulled behind a car by a rope while he was on fire—he was being *dragged down the street on fire*. That's probably the craziest thing that I've ever seen in my life. It almost felt like a dream.

I've also seen people I went to high school with go to prison. I've had one of my best friends turn into a drug addict. I've also fallen out with friends I thought would be with me for life because we didn't see eye to eye on my achieving goals and them feeling entitled to a certain lifestyle. Being overwhelmed by actually achieving some of my dreams and realizing that there's way more to it than I had imagined drove me to a bad place psychologically. I thought I was handling those things well enough that I was doing okay, but what I learned from therapy is that the goal isn't to be "okay." The goal is to continue to become better.

I know that I still have a long way to go when it comes to my growth. Growth is a cyclical thing. The objective isn't to become perfect; it's to keep working on yourself continuously. You go through all these steps, and once you get to the last step, it's not like life is all figured out. You have to go back around, but you're going to do it from a different perspective. You will become someone who's seen the miracle of working on yourself and the solutions and happiness that it brings, the productivity and sense of accomplishment that you feel.

I'm getting back into therapy after being out of it for a year or two. I loved my therapist, and I thought that our time had come to an end after a year of working together. But then I found that I missed it, so I went back.

Going in and out of therapy over the years stemmed from listening to myself and knowing it's never bad to ask for help or talk things through. I talk to friends and mentors, too, but they don't fully substitute for a professional. It's always good to be able to talk through issues with someone who isn't your friend or your family member because they can be more objective, and you're better able to leave whatever you talk about there instead of bringing it home with you.

The act of communicating and talking translates to greater health in every single one of your relationships in life, whether it's business, romantic, personal, family, friendship, or with yourself. It's good to communicate with someone when it's their job to know how to listen well and to help you think about things in a new way. You're not here on this earth by yourself. You're here with eight billion other people, and some of those people can really relate to you. Everything is an interaction. The teacher learns from the student. It's never just a one-way thing, and that's the beauty of life.

When I leave my therapist's office, I feel so much lighter because I've been able to unpack so much and leave it there. Sometimes, if you unload all that on a family member or a friend you see all the time, they are then left with that; now they may have to carry that baggage around. That may strengthen a relationship, but it could also weaken a relationship. It could be inconsiderate because you're dumping so much on someone who has their own life, too. You always have to be conscious that everyone is going through something.

If you don't like the first therapist you meet with, you don't have to stick with them. Ask friends for recommendations, or your doctor, or your insurance company. Read reviews online. There are multiple online therapy apps that are easy to use. It's completely fine to shop around before you settle on someone. To those who have sought therapy and didn't get the kind of help they wanted: Don't give up. Find someone else, another person who relates to you more. Don't abandon the concept and think you don't need it just because you see one therapist and it doesn't work. It's like finding the right barber or a favorite restaurant. You have to experiment sometimes, and that's part of working on yourself.

And even when you find someone you like, you don't always have to take the therapist's truth as the full truth. That's the thing about therapy: it's a human interaction, and sometimes what is said in that room applies to you and sometimes it doesn't. Take the grain of salt and add it to your plate of food. No matter who says what, there is no right or wrong way to live your life. It's a matter of perspective. I think people are sometimes scared of therapy because it's something they may not fully understand. But in my experience most therapists are just wise guides supporting you as you do the work of better understanding yourself.

When someone suggests "You should do therapy," I don't get offended like I used to. A while ago, my ego would have said, "What do you mean I need therapy? Maybe *you* need therapy!" Now I think, *Huh. What are they seeing that I might not be aware of yet? Is there information in what they're telling me about myself that I can use to become better in the world and within myself? Probably so.*

This latest time I went back into therapy because I was feeling overwhelmed. I needed to take some of that weight off and leave it in the therapist's office.

You can go without a reason, too. Curiosity is reason enough to **try** it out and see how it works for you. I encourage everyone to **try** therapy. It's safe to say that pretty much everyone would benefit from it. Therapy is a time to say your thoughts out loud, to self-actualize, to sit with yourself. We're living in a world where we're online constantly, engaging with phones and computers that are throwing ideas and points of comparison at us. It's very easy to lose ourselves because there's so much clutter. I think therapy is something that helps you keep a grip on yourself, to tune into you and not what everyone else is going on about or what the world is going through.

If you've done therapy, what have you learned from it? If you've never done it, what's your hesitation? If you think about doing it, what would you want to talk about?

Handwritten things always feel more personal to me.

CHAPTER ELEVEN
Journaling

▪ *trying*

I FIND JOURNALING TO BE a great way to fight anxiety. Usually anxiety is this nagging feeling that something is wrong or that something is going to go wrong in the future. When you journal, you're able to write through the moods and the things that are eating at you or let them go without assigning meaning to them. This way, you can eventually figure out why you're feeling the way you're feeling. Putting a name to a feeling tends to be one of the best ways to get control over it. I also like to read my journal entries out loud. Something about saying it out loud seems to activate it more. Even reading it over and saying it out loud in your head makes a difference.

You might ask yourself, *Why do I want to journal?* You don't journal because you feel like you're supposed to do it. You journal because it benefits you or maybe reminds you of something or helps you to look back on your week, or perhaps creates something you will be able to look at thirty years from now and know where your mind was.

You can journal like that, explaining where you are in life, talking about your day, how you feel at the moment, how your last day, month, or year was. I think it's a cool way of checking in with yourself. You shouldn't feel pressure to write beautifully. This isn't for anyone else to see—just you.

Most of the time I'm doing gratitude journaling, so I'm saying what I'm thankful for and writing down things that I want to apply to my life. I'm empowering myself, hyping myself up. I write down my agreements and affirmations, but this is a place where there are no rules. I can say whatever I want, work through questions, make lists—anything that helps me get what's in my mind onto the page, where it starts to make more sense and feel less overwhelming. When you write whatever's on your mind and let your mind go free, you learn so much about what you're thinking and how you're thinking about it.

Sometimes, I write something describing the day. For example, "I am happy to celebrate my brother's birthday today." There are going to be times in my life when I probably will want to look back through my journal to see how I've **manifested** my goals. But the main goal of journaling is to momentarily focus 100 percent on yourself and how you're feeling. It's a lot like therapy, except you can do it on your own anytime, and it's free!

To me, writing in a journal is a form of meditation, like going on a hike. Some people go on the hiking trail and sprint super-fast, and they're sweating. Some people take their sweet time walking on the trail. Sometimes I take my sweet time! Sometimes I'm doing it for a workout. Sometimes I'm doing it to clear my mind. Sometimes I'm doing it to see nature, to stop and look at snails on the ground or birds in the sky.

I have a gold journal because gold feels heavenly. It feels like the right energy for thinking through things on a higher plane. I usually have a gold pen, and I write in blue ink because, to me, blue is the color of power. Now, if I'm somewhere and I lose my pen and I only have a black pen, I'll work with a black pen. If I don't have my journal and I still want to write stuff down, I'll write it on a piece of paper. But ideally, I always have my gold journal and my gold pen with blue ink in it.

When I was going through a challenging time, my mom reached out to Marie Diamond, with whom she was taking an online feng shui class, and said, "My son could use your expertise and help getting aligned." She replied and said, "*My* son has Sean on his vision board! I think this is a sign!"

Marie came to meet with me at my house in LA, and it felt like seeing a long-lost friend or someone from a past life. There was a familiarity, even though we don't have that much in common. We immediately hit it off as pals. She's helped me out a lot over the years.

I always thought feng shui was about arranging and decorating your house or office, but it's really about the arrangement of your whole life. Of course, fixing my environment is important, but I also needed to take a look at the organization of everything around me. She taught me about how important it is to face certain directions for certain activities.

She even has an app now that she's named after herself. You can personalize a profile that includes a compass that shows you what directions are best for you for your health, success, and wisdom, all by using the date and time of your birth. I was skeptical at first, until I actually applied it and saw a difference firsthand. I find that looking at it helps me think about what will give me a higher chance of being a better version of myself.

My success direction is south, my wisdom direction is east, and my health direction is north. So, in the studio, I have things facing in my success direction. If I'm in the gym, I like working out in my health direction. If I'm meditating, I like to meditate either in my success direction or my wisdom direction.

I used to journal in whatever journals I had around, but Marie suggested that, for feng shui purposes, I work with colors. I've always heard the saying that the pen is mightier than the sword. She said, "You should have a gold pen so that it's like a sword to you." That sounded right, and I started using gold pens. I do things that work for me, whether or not they sound silly to other people.

There are some days when I don't get to do it. Some days are so busy that I wake up and have to immediately get to work, or I wake up late and skip it. But I'll usually catch up with my journal the next day. Routine is important to enhance these activities. It's easy to get out of the habit if you don't constantly reinforce this work.

I go through phases when I feel a lot of heaviness—say, when I'm moving a lot and haven't been taking much time to relax. That can leave me a little drained. Keeping up with journaling reminds me that I'm in control of how I feel.

Journaling has allowed me to understand myself better. It shows me my repeated behavioral patterns and lets me take a look outside myself and think about why I do the things I do over and over again. It's a great way to get intrusive thoughts out of my head and cut them off from their power.

I encourage you to **try** all forms of journaling that appeal until you find what works best for you. There's no right or wrong way to journal.

The cosmic realm works for you, within you. When you feel bad, know it's because you're not in alignment with who you truly are or you're not living up to your potential and know you can do better. There's a silver lining in that. That's where you see the possibility. I've found it helpful to write my way through these moments of discomfort.

Get a journal and a pen that feel special to you. Take ten minutes a day to write through thoughts and feelings you're having, or goals and questions you have about your life, or just free-associate and write anything that comes into your mind. There's no wrong way to do this. After two weeks, read over what you've written and see what surprises you, and see if the way you're thinking about your life has grown deeper or changed in some way.

The only way to meditate wrong is to not do it.

CHAPTER TWELVE
Meditating

▪ *trying, manifesting*

THERE'S NO RIGHT OR WRONG way to meditate. What's important is that you **try** it and use it to work on **manifesting** your most beautiful future.

I've developed my method of meditation from books I've read and my work with therapists and spiritual leaders throughout my life. Over time, I've found that different meditations activate different areas of my brain, and that I like to meditate wherever I am—whether that's while falling asleep, showering, or sitting quietly in nature. I personally only meditate for thirty minutes maximum. I usually do ten to fifteen minutes. If I'm going through an intense time, I may meditate twice a day. But to me, it's not like the longer you do it, the more benefit it has. The main purpose of it is to better serve the rest of your day. You get in the meditative state in order to be more present in your life; you don't skip big parts of your life in order to meditate.

When it comes to meditating, many people have an idea that it's intimidating, like you have to be a Zen master, able to calm your mind and keep it blank. I've had friends say, "I could never meditate! I can't turn my brain off. It's always running."

But you don't have to turn off your brain. Meditation is just taking the conscious time out to be still and connect with yourself. You really can't do it wrong; it's not possible. Even if your mind races, the fact that you took the time out to be still or bring your mind back to a central thought or take time off from your phone or focus on your breathing means you're doing so much more for yourself than you realize.

I like to journal before I meditate because it puts me in that mind frame, like spiritual foreplay. I might write down an intention or a gratitude. Then I close my journal and close my eyes. I like to start by taking a deep breath and imagining that I'm somewhere in nature (if I'm not actually there). In my mind, I like to go to a couple of beautiful spots in California—Zuma Beach or Mount Shasta—or the South of France. I imagine I'm there, and the sun is shining on me.

As I take a deep breath in and exhale a deep breath out, I'll count to one, two, three, four; then, on the fifth count, I start exhaling: one, two, three, four, five. Other people like to use "box breathing." That means you breathe in for a count of four, hold your breath for a count of four, breathe out for a count of four, and rest for a count of four.

I imagine with every inhale and exhale that I'm surrounded by the light of creation, which to me is the same as the light from the sun that gives life to earth and makes things bloom. I imagine it entering my body from above my head, pouring into me. I invite that light to replace anything that's negative, anything that doesn't match the vibration of the light and the energy of the universe. I invite it to leave my body through my feet and go back to the earth. I imagine that light filling up every cell of my body, every organ, every piece of me.

I think of what's been bothering me in my life, and I pretend I'm in a shower of light and it's washing all those things away.

Once I feel the gunk has been cleared away, which usually takes about a minute or two max, I imagine that a protective barrier forms around me. I imagine this bubble as royal blue because, like I've said, for me, that's the color of power. I tell myself that whatever I'm working on, I have the power to accomplish it.

Then I imagine myself surrounded in a bubble of rose, which represents the unconditional love of the whole universe. I give thanks to the universe for supporting me and bringing me to where I am.

Finally, I picture anything that's hindering me, whether that's an obstacle or a feeling of guilt, being completely disintegrated. I've read that purple is the color of forgiving, so I imagine a violet flame that burns away things that are holding me back or that I need to let go of.

Then I rub my hands together, to feel the sensation of creating heat through friction, and put them over my eyes. Then I open my eyes and bring myself back into the moment.

Again, all that takes only about ten or fifteen minutes. I feel like the main thing is taking the time off for yourself and paying attention to your body and your breath. Sometimes it takes multiple meditations over time to develop the habit, but it always happens eventually. Some of my greatest inspirations—like Kobe Bryant, Jay Z, and many others—have meditated frequently and believed it was one of the most essential habits to include in a routine. It's been scientifically proven to improve your brain function and health as well, so this isn't just some woo-woo stuff. If you plan on being the most successful you, the happiest and richest version of yourself, I suggest you begin replacing at least fifteen minutes of screen time with meditation and/or journaling to energize your mind.

Guided Meditation

Take ten minutes right now and try this meditation exercise. Close your eyes, and in your mind, try to go to a place in nature (a beach, a forest, the top of a hill) where you feel safe and relaxed. Imagine yourself being bathed in the golden light of creation, the light of the universe, and imagine it washing away any feelings you don't want to feel anymore, like dirt being washed away in the shower. Then protect that energy by envisioning the power of the universe protecting you. I like to imagine this as a royal blue light surrounding the golden light I built up. After that, I welcome the love and support of God or the universe (use whatever you believe in) to show up and support me fully in my pursuits. Lastly, I envision a violet flame, said to be the energy of forgiveness. This burns away all that is holding me back, whether it's an old belief or pattern or a blockage. Imagine the violet flame flowing through you, burning away all that is no longer needed. After that, connect with your higher self, which you can picture at an arm's length or so above you. Feel the light, love, and protection of the universe aligned with yourself and attracting the very things you desire like a magnet. Then you're ready to go!

This is just how I do my meditation. There are many meditations available online, whether Oprah and Deepak's thirty-day guided meditations or great ones on apps like Headspace, Calm, and tons of others. These are all excellent ways to get started on your meditation journey.

There's no right or wrong way to do any of this. Try this once a day and see what's most useful, what changes, what difference it makes to the rest of your day. Over the next couple of weeks, try it out ten times, for a hundred minutes total, before you decide whether or not it works for you.

When you go outside, you can see that every living thing, including us, is part of the same life force—meaning we are made from that same beautiful energy and are all interconnected.

CHAPTER THIRTEEN
Getting Outside

accepting, trusting

IT WASN'T UNTIL I WAS a full-blown adult that I took a trip by myself that was not for work. I needed to clear my head, so I drove up alone to Big Sur.

Not long after I arrived, I got a text from a friend: "Hey, who are you up there with?"

"I'm here solo, came up here to clear my mind," I said.

My friend wrote back: "If you want to go on a great hike, I have two friends up there who are professional hikers."

I hit them up, and they invited me on a hike. They offered me a microdose of LSD. I never would have done that, except they were so sweet and so cool. I only took a little bit, but it probably made me more fearless than I would have been otherwise. Right away, they had me hopping over a DO NOT ENTER sign hanging from a chain blocking a particular trail.

We walked along for a while, and it was all fine, but then we came to a tree that had been hit by lightning and was blocking our way. To get past it, we had to swing from another tree over a chasm, Tarzan-style. (For the record, I don't advise dropping acid and hopping over holes in the earth.)

"We've done it before," they said. "It's not hard, promise!"

I was looking at the edge of the cliff—a cliff that if you fell off it, you could die.

The wife did it first, and her husband told me, "I'll go after you. I can catch you if something goes wrong."

I jumped. The swinging part was fine, but then I forgot to let go of the branch. The husband helped stop me, and it was all okay, but five minutes later, he said, "I'm not gonna lie. I was pretty worried about you back there."

I hadn't been worried about it until that moment, but then I was!

I'd still always rather have days like that than to stay home safe and never get fresh air. Walking outside in nature brings me back to the moment and helps me feel grounded. I love hiking, but even if there isn't time for that, it's usually possible to step outside for a few minutes, where I can be by myself and focus on taking deep breaths, expanding my lungs. I do that a few times, relax, and analyze how I'm feeling.

I know some of us live in a concrete jungle where nature isn't so prevalent, and some of us live in neighborhoods where it's not so safe to wander outside. When that's the case, I would suggest imagining yourself in nature, because the subconscious mind can barely tell the difference.

If I have heaviness, I acknowledge it. Sometimes I don't recognize why I'm so overwhelmed or why I'm stressed out. But when I take the time to breathe, I can figure it out. When I figure out where the negative feelings are coming from, I say, "I return this energy to the earth with light and love attached to it." I envision the earth transforming all that stress and heaviness into oxygen. I feel a difference after I do that.

When I walk outside, I ask myself questions: *What is it that's stopping me from realizing my full potential? What is it that's stopping me from going higher? What is it that's holding me back when I feel this heaviness? Let it be identified.*

Spiritual speaker and energy healer Christie Marie Sheldon promotes this line of questioning. She says we should identify the source of the heaviness and then say, "I clear, delete, destroy, and transmute this energy across all time, dimensions, space, and realities." It's a little deep, but it works very well.

That alone is a way of grounding yourself, but I find it's more powerful out in the natural world. I recommend taking off your shoes and socks and feeling your feet on the ground. If you're not able to get to nature in the real world, then imagine yourself with your feet in the sand or dirt or in the ocean. Imagine that the light is flowing through you and that your feet are planted and that your energy is going all the way to the center of the earth, where the earth has its own soul.

I know it sounds wacky. But you can always benefit from taking a moment in the natural world to ground yourself, or at least picture the world holding you and matching your light with its light. When I see the sunlight, I remember that it gives life to plants and also sustains me, and that whatever else is happening, every day the sun is there, and we are being nurtured by it.

The next time you find yourself feeling upset or confused or heavy, find a way to spend a few minutes out in nature, taking a few deep breaths. Imagine your energy going down into the center of the earth.

People who are on the same wavelength will often **manifest** in one another's lives.

CHAPTER FOURTEEN
Finding Role Models

▪ *strategizing, manifesting*

WHEN CHOOSING A ROLE MODEL, someone to look up to and emulate, you need to pick someone who aligns with you. It doesn't have to be a famous person. It doesn't have to be a super-deep person. It could be a coworker, a boss, a friend, a parent, a grandparent—really whoever. There are no rules.

But there's another option when picking someone, and that's choosing someone you know about but don't personally know. One of the best parts about living in this day and age is that you can find people you think of as your guides or mentors who you don't even know in real life. When you read about them online, you can usually learn a lot, and you can actually apply the lessons they teach to your life. It doesn't have to be someone you could ever study from directly. But if you find them interesting, you can study their work, their books, their interviews, their music, whatever it is they do, and you can get on their wavelength and create an energetic bond.

Deepak Chopra was somebody I really attached to. I admire his philosophy and how he thinks. You can create an energetic bond with someone who isn't in your life and find ways to learn from them. I've watched a lot of Denzel Washington interviews because I love what he puts out. He always drops gems and cool quotes and concepts to live by. He gives a great perspective as a Black man who's navigated this industry for most of his life. He was also in an acting class in New York with my mom! I got to sit down and talk to him in person once, along with Lenny Kravitz, outside a WME party, and it was one of the most memorable conversations of my life. I was in shock so I don't remember a lot of details. I was just thinking, *This is crazy! Kicking it with Denzel!*

You might actually meet the people you follow, though that's not necessary when it comes to studying them and making them a presence in your life. While it's not the goal, it's true that people who are on the same vibration and wavelength will often **manifest** in each other's life. They will attract each other like a magnet.

And yet it's not always the best outcome. I have many friends who have met their role models and have been crushed by the reality of that person being someone they don't get along with or actually see eye to eye with on a lot of things, so make sure that you're prepared. If you actually meet your role model, whoever it is in your life, make sure you have no expectations of that person, because you don't want to get your hopes shattered.

I'm sure I've disappointed a fan in my time, but I work hard to be present whenever I can be. There was one kid in Colorado I think about a lot. I was headlining a sold-out tour, and this kid waited outside my bus all day in the cold. I went and did a radio spot, and when I came back, he was still out there. My manager said, "I think you've got to meet this kid. He's dressed like you. And he can't be older than thirteen."

We brought him on the bus, and he was going crazy, he was so happy. We gave him a ticket to the show. After it was over, he came back to my dressing room, crying, and said, "I just want to make a better life for my mom like you did for yours, man."

He showed me pictures on his phone from his birthday party. He had a Big Sean cake. It was a good reminder that having a microphone means that you have an opportunity to change people's lives.

That was a nice moment for that kid and me, but I'd like to think he still would have gotten what he needed from my music even if we'd never met. You can learn so much from what people put out in the world. They can guide you wherever they are and wherever you are.

With the Sean Anderson Foundation, we help a lot of kids through after-school programs, and we linked kids with pen pals from schools on the west side of Detroit to Soweto, South Africa. They wrote each other and shared experiences as part of something called Project Knapsack. Every summer, in partnership with the Boys and Girls Clubs of Southeast Michigan, we set up stations in the inner city where kids can learn how to meditate, get free haircuts and free braiding, learn how to set up YouTube and gaming pages, and have mental health talks. We set up carnival games and performances. The community really comes together.

Giving back can change somebody's life, change somebody's trajectory, inspire them. You never know how you're impacting somebody just with your presence. And yet, "legacy" is something that you really shouldn't think about. You should just focus on doing your best, and the legacy part is something that takes care of itself. If you do things for your legacy, you might not be doing them for the right reasons.

A true legacy comes from your putting your best foot forward and not thinking too far beyond that. You're going to leave a legacy no matter what, whether it's a historical career or a beautiful healthy baby you've raised, whether it's a friend you helped out or just being a happy person and spreading that vibration. That's more important to me than winning a hundred awards. Just being happy is the most important thing. Otherwise, what's the point of even existing?

One of the most positive people I've ever met is Stevie Wonder. He's become a good friend of mine, which is really cool to be able to say! I've been in the studio with him a few times, and he actually did a skit on my fifth album, where he talked about Detroit and his experience there. To me, he is the greatest singer-songwriter of all time, the GOAT. But even cooler is that he has such a happy personality. He's changed lives with his joy.

That happiness starts within, and then you expand it to your family, then your block, then your neighborhood, then to the city, then to the state, then the country, and then the world, and it keeps expanding. It's like a chain reaction, and it all starts with your doing the work. Self-work is so important because it's the first step to changing the world. You never know how one interaction can change the course of somebody's life to the extent that they could be a leader of the world one day. A minor change of perspective can have major ripple effects. That's why we need to be careful about whose influence we take in, and how we influence other people.

Who would you like to take on as your role model? How can you learn more about how they think? What do you think you might get out of an energetic bond with that person?

No matter what, time with quality people is productive, sometimes without my even realizing it.

CHAPTER FIFTEEN

Healthy Friendships

▪ *trying, manifesting*

A "GOOD FRIEND" TO ME is a funny label. I feel like a friend is a friend is a friend. They're all good or they're not real friendships. To me, friends are people you connect with and who are supportive of you, though not blindly supportive. In a healthy give-and-take, they question you and inspire you in different ways or bring out certain sides of you that you may not have found on your own.

There are lots of times when we lose sight of the meaning of friendship because we get close to the wrong people and suddenly find ourselves saying, "Wait! How can this person be my friend and treat me poorly?" The obvious answer: That's not your friend. That was an imposter, somebody who was infiltrating your heart.

Friendships don't always last forever. There may be people you are friends with at a certain time in life, but as you change and evolve as a person, you may not connect with them anymore. You may no longer energetically be on the same path or the same vibration that you used to be. That's all right, too. Your life changes and progresses. You don't have to feel guilty about your needs or your timeline. There are times when I don't see people I care about for a year or two, but when we get back together, it's like we haven't missed a beat because we're real friends.

It took a lot of **trying** and **manifesting** to get the right people into my life. Once we're able to clearly articulate our needs, I find that so often people magically pop up to lead us into a new phase in our lives where those things are possible.

I'm so thankful for my friendships. There's the saying "You are the company you keep." I've looked around rooms and felt, *Man, these are the people I love being around.* Whether I see them every week or once a year, the bond is absolute.

My friend Mike Posner is a great example of that. We can go so long without seeing each other and then after an hour or two it's like we haven't missed anything. I brought him out at Coachella not too long ago, and it was a great full-circle moment from us writing music in his mom's basement and playing college shows and frat parties together to sharing a stage on one of the biggest platforms. After all we've seen and been through together, that was a dream come true.

I have a few great friends like that, and I know that no matter what, we've got each other's backs. I also like being around people I consider to be masters of their craft and can learn from as well. I consider a lot of those people friends, too, especially based on experiences we've had or work we've done together. I enjoy our meaningful interactions. It's a lot different than it is with my best friends, though.

Time with good people is usually productive, sometimes without my even realizing it. I know people who avoid socializing because they work all the time, but the truth is that some of my best ideas have come from hanging out, thinking I was off the clock. And even though

I don't like conflict in my personal relationships, I've often found that disagreements have helped me learn something about what I desire or need.

One of my challenges is to work through hard times with the people in my life without becoming defensive. I need to show up to learn what I'm meant to learn from that relationship. I've come to believe that defensiveness is like putting yourself on a pedestal and saying, "I'm better than you. You're wrong." As soon as I feel myself thinking that way, I stop and remember that putting up walls stops you from growing. To cast someone out without reflection is like locking a door without checking to see who's on the other side.

In my friendships, we try to make each other better, share information, and be nonjudgmental with each other, to remember we're all just doing what we can. I personally love hyping my friends up and cheering them on, and I really appreciate when they return that same energy to me as well. Ultimately, your deepest lifelong friendship is with yourself—so don't forget to hype yourself up, and recognize that the people who support that relationship are the ones to keep around, nurture, and appreciate.

I know there are some of us who don't like ourselves for a lot of different reasons and struggle with being in our own skin. I've been there before, too. I think it's important to recognize that today is a new day and to forgive yourself for being human. That feeling is just an indication that you can do better and are meant for more. Some of the tools mentioned earlier (meditation, journaling, trying new experiences, etc.) aren't just ways to work on yourself but also ways to work on loving yourself. You're never alone in your feelings.

Are you surrounding yourself with people who reflect your values and make you a better version of yourself? Are you a good friend to others? What are the characteristics that make a good friend? How can you be a better friend to yourself? (Once in a while, I take myself out for dinner or go to the movies by myself.)

You're gonna be a much happier person when you stop assuming.

CHAPTER SIXTEEN
Never Assume

■ *accepting, trying, trusting*

ONE OF THE GREATEST CHALLENGES in romantic relationships is to **accept** who's sitting in front of us, not some fantasy of who our partner is. The best way to find clarity is to communicate openly rather than playing games or making assumptions. It's about facing the truth and appreciating what's good about it rather than approaching things with some preconceived idea about how people should be.

It's not like I haven't messed things up or crossed lines I shouldn't have. I for sure am no saint, and I don't want to make it seem one-sided. But I have learned and grown from a lot of my previous relationships, and sometimes since then I've broken a rule without even knowing the rule was there. For example, I had a girlfriend who got mad at me for liking the Instagram photos of other women whose accounts I followed. I wasn't hitting on them or anything obviously objectionable.

She acted like I should have known that it was wrong to click "like" if it was a woman's post, and like it was even suspicious to have women friends on social media. But I had no idea she felt that way about likes! Once I knew, I could decide whether I wanted to change how I acted online, or we could discuss where our boundaries were around all that. But until she shared her feelings openly, I had no way of knowing that was something she expected. To me, it's important to be explicit about what's okay or not okay.

We're all capable of spiraling into fear or doubt, telling stories about what's happening, inventing problems. I've learned that a person's ego or pride can sometimes be hurt by something you may not think of as a big deal. What's important is to **try** to look clearly at the person in front of you. Share how you're feeling and what you're seeing. Approach your own feelings and the other person's with curiosity. Be open to learning more about yourself and your partner. One of the hardest things to do in the heat of the moment, I've realized, is to step outside your perspective and understand your partner's perspective. I feel like a place of understanding is always a pathway to a solution. That doesn't mean you have to agree with their perspective, but at least acknowledging it shows that you care.

One person I was once in a relationship with told me she liked that I was friendly. I hold the door for everyone. I compliment people, guys and girls. I'll say, "Hey, I love that shirt," or, "Man, those shoes are cool." Not all the time, but if something speaks to me, I'll say it because that's how I feel. I believe that giving someone a compliment can be a gift. You never know how much that may mean to somebody. I figured it never hurts.

That was one of the things this person said she loved about me when we were first dating. And then, once we were in a relationship and she saw that was how I still treated everyone, she said, "Wait— you're *too* nice," or, if I said something positive about a female friend, "Why are you complimenting other women?"

I said, "But that's how I've always been. That's one of the reasons you liked me in the first place."

The way I saw it, it was assumed that things had to be different instead of communicating that first. I've also been on the other side of this concept as well. I thought my partner should do things a certain way. But again, where the ball gets dropped is when we're not communicating our expectations. Sometimes we don't want to bring up hard things due to incredible chemistry or great times. But in order to keep things good we need to express what it is we desire from the relationship. Boundaries have to be discussed and negotiated before they can be enforced. Feelings aren't rules.

One of the most exciting things in my life has been becoming a parent. Noah's mom and I are in several relationships with each other all at once. We're peers. We have a music project together. We were friends for five or six years before we started dating. Collaborating with her has always been a joy of mine. That doesn't mean we don't get irritated with each other over the smallest things sometimes. She takes after her grandfather, who was a lawyer, and is an amazing debater. She'd have made a good lawyer, and I've learned a lot from her—like how to pay a lot of attention to what I say!

Some roles come easier to me than others, and the way I get better is by listening carefully and by showing up and being honest. Often that means having difficult, even painful, conversations. Too many of us don't stop to ask questions until we're unhappy. For so long, we say, "Oh, it's lovey-dovey, it's amazing, it's butterflies." And to keep that fantasy of perfection going, we ignore static or red flags. There may be things the other person says that you don't agree with, but you think, *I can probably get over that. Better not to rock the boat.* (Well, that's what I think. Some of you don't mind tipping that boat all the way over!) But those are things that can also tear you apart later on. If they're not addressed, those little things can turn into big things.

The best way to build a strong, honest foundation in a relationship is to operate in good faith, **trust** in the basic goodness of each other, and communicate well. One of the benefits of working on yourself and knowing who you are is that you can then express that to the other person. To me, learning how to love yourself comes down to doing things that make you happy and knowing what's best for you, so long as it's not detrimental to your loved ones.

When you're vibrating on a certain level, what you want is also going to be attracted to you. I know so many people who wanted to find a partner in life, but it wasn't until they figured out the rest of their life and found peace within themselves that they finally met someone who was a good fit.

When I've had breakups, I think the main reason was that it wasn't working for either of us. It was becoming more of a burden than a gift. When you're not right with yourself, you can't be the best partner. Showing up as your best self to any relationship is key, whether that's personally or professionally. Because that's what you have to offer. That's why I do self-care work like journaling, meditating, and therapy. Your whole life is relationships. And the common denominator in all of them is you. You're in a relationship with yourself for as long as you live.

If you're with someone, make a list of everything you would like to see in your relationship. What do you agree on? Are there any surprises?

If you're not in a relationship, make a list of everything you'd love to have in a partner and start attracting that to yourself.

Everybody's going through something.

CHAPTER SEVENTEEN

What You're Running from Can Save You

▪ *accepting, trusting*

FOR YEARS, I DIDN'T FEEL ready to have a baby, but my partner was, so I went along with the plan. When we first got pregnant, there was a miscarriage. Apparently, this type of miscarriage is common—a "blighted ovum," where the embryo keeps growing but the gestational sac is empty. When I first heard that, it sounded crazy to me—a fetus that's empty inside.

It was rough. And I blamed myself. I imagined that this feeling I had of not being sure if I was ready for a baby somehow contributed to it not working out.

I know that's not how miscarriages work, but I still felt it. Miscarriage is such a taboo topic, and when we don't talk openly about things, it contributes to people feeling alone when they go through them. Men tend not to discuss their experiences around becoming fathers or around pregnancy loss. You want to say the right thing and be supportive, but you may have complicated feelings, and you might end up saying the wrong thing.

I had a childish reaction when she first told me she was pregnant. I said I wasn't ready. I knew having a child was a blessing, but I didn't know that it was right for me because I'd never had a child of my own and seen the magnificence. I couldn't fathom it. That was how I honestly felt. But I look back and regret saying I wasn't ready out loud in that moment. I wasn't being considerate, and that may have just been a reactionary response. We were on two different pages. I look back on that now, wishing I had had a little bit more awareness at that time in my life.

I asked my partner, "Are you sure you want to do this? Are you sure we're ready?"

I wish I'd hugged her instead and said, "Yes! Thank God!"

Ultimately, I realized that I was as ready as I'd ever be for a baby, and then God blessed us with another pregnancy. Now that we have Noah, I realize how much of a miracle it is to even have a baby make it through all the stages of pregnancy and the magic a baby brings when it's born. Before that, I knew kids were very special, and I had always wanted them in theory, but I never said, "Okay, now is the time to have kids."

This was a huge life change, and one about which I had serious preconceived notions. I put a lot of pressure on myself. *Make sure it's the right person. Make sure it's the right time. Make sure you have plenty of money. Don't be too young. Don't be too old.* Instead, I should have let God guide it.

It takes depth and vulnerability to go within yourself and to **accept** your complicated feelings on your way to finding stillness. You have to make yourself a priority and be gentle with yourself. When it comes to feelings, there's no good or bad. You just have to feel the feelings and know when they're showing you something, allowing them to come and go. It's a blessing to be able to feel these things. But it's also important to **trust** that your fear might not be the whole story. I can think of many times when I was running from something that ended up being exactly what I needed in order to grow and become a better version of myself.

I wrote a song that mentioned losing the pregnancy, and some people were shocked. It's not usually something people talk about in songs. But I feel like being vulnerable in music is what you're supposed to do as an artist. I like to talk about what I go through, and I find it's often what other people are going through, too. It makes me feel less alone.

Not one of us has a perfect life or always acts perfectly. I believe that if we did, we'd have passed on to the next level and wouldn't be on this earth. I was running from the idea of having a family because of a false narrative I'd built up in my head about what and who I had to be. My partner already had a daughter, and I wondered whether I was up to the challenge of functioning as a parental figure to a teenager. When I was younger, I used to say, "I'll never date someone who has a kid." But her daughter and I have an awesome bond. She's a really cool person. I love hearing her perspective on things. I take pride in being another male figure in addition to her dad, who's there for her and who she can talk to.

My son's mom has a very big family, and I have a small family. I like the balance of it all and how we deal with things differently, and how good it seems for Noah. The thing that matters most to me is being close to him. His face lights up when he sees his family together. I believe he can feel the love from all of us, and we definitely feel it from him.

What are you avoiding in your life? Is it possible that this thing might serve you in your development? What's the best that could happen from it?

Whatever you put out into the universe comes back at you.

CHAPTER EIGHTEEN
Being Kind

▪ *trying*

I LEARNED A LOT ABOUT being good to people from Pharrell Williams. I met him at the beginning of my career. We were in Japan, and I was doing a photoshoot for the twentieth anniversary of the legendary streetwear clothing line started by Tomoaki Nagao (Nigo), A Bathing Ape (BAPE).

Pharrell was BAPE's brand ambassador, and it was my favorite brand at the time. He and I got to talking and realized we connected on a lot of things. We became friends. The first time I went to the studio with him, he was talking to the person who was sweeping up and giving him the exact same respect as a superstar. I saw him taking the time to know everyone, no matter who they were.

When I commented on how cool I thought that was, he told me that he treats all people with the same respect, that he doesn't believe in anyone being better than anyone else. That's something that I took from him. I had never really belittled anybody before, but he helped to instill in me a foundation of treating all human beings with full attention.

Not that you do it to get something, but treating people well does rebound to you. I recently had someone say, "Eight years ago, you were so easy to work with, so on time, so professional, so caring and kind. That's why we booked you again."

I didn't remember the shoot they were talking about, but I took that as confirmation that every single day, every single interaction, and every single chance you get is building up your reputation. The best way to do this is to sincerely respect other people and put good wishes out into the universe for them.

How can you do this, I'm often asked, when people can be annoying or hostile?

Well, once you realize that you're in control of your own feelings, you're able to get over negative emotions at a much more rapid rate. I've learned to say, "Man, hold on. Let me go through how I'm feeling and let me recognize that this is temporary. I will get past this. And not only will I get past it but I'll also get past it as a better version of myself for having gone through this. I'm in control of my emotions."

Every time I get into a heated situation, I think that and cool down immediately. I don't get worked up like I used to. I'll just say, "Look, I understand where you're coming from, but I don't feel that way." And then, "I see you, though. I want to let you know that I see you."

Holding on to anger or a grudge can be a very heavy thing to bear, even if you don't realize it. It's like holding a glass of water. It's not heavy, but if you hold it up all day long, you're going to be sweating and your arm is going to feel like it's about to fall off. That's how it is with the little things we hold on to. One of the easiest ways to metaphorically put the glass down is to do the work to understand.

I **try** to always come from a place of understanding. And I also **try** not to suggest that anything someone else feels is invalid. Everyone's feelings are valid. You never want to make anyone feel like you don't understand them. That's how arguments within relationships happen. How many fights happen because someone feels unseen or unheard? That's how conflict occurs. It's a lack of understanding and letting your ego control you.

All other human beings are fellow travelers on this earth, with their own challenges and gifts, and so I always wish good things for everyone. I believe that whatever you put out into the universe comes back at you. When you compliment someone or say a prayer for them, that's good karma for you, regardless of whether or not they reciprocate your good wishes.

After I've met someone and had a genuine interaction with them, I often walk away and say to the universe, "Man, I really hope that the best comes to that person," or, "I really hope they have an amazing life."

I wish it for their sake, and for my own. You're giving yourself a true gift to wish good things for someone else, and it doesn't cost anything. It comes back to you in ways you can't imagine. That's the way the universe works. I don't expect people to compliment me all the time or tell me good things, but when it does come to me, I receive it gladly.

Once a day for the next week, wish something good for someone after spending a moment with them. It could be a child, a friend, a bank teller—someone you love or someone you barely know. Maybe even say it for someone you don't particularly like, such as someone who's cut you off in traffic. Just take a couple of seconds to honor them with a little prayer that they will have some goodness in their life.

I used to try to over-understand until I understood that overthinking was underwhelming and mainly my wanting to control things I couldn't control. Sometimes you have to let go and get a grip. Life is unpredictable.

CHAPTER NINETEEN
Letting People Go

▪ *accepting, trusting*

I HAVE A HIT SONG called "I Don't Fuck with You." It's about drawing a line in terms of what you will and won't put up with. It's also about feeling unfulfilled and refusing to spend any more time with something or someone that no longer serves you.

There have been people I've had to reject and turn away from in that way. I always want to have a forgiving heart, but sometimes people aren't on the same page as you. You can forgive someone, and they can hurt you again. So you have to set your boundaries. That's something that I've learned a lot of times the hard way.

A lot of people assumed that song was about breaking up with an ex-girlfriend of mine. Mainly, it was about breaking up and letting go. While I've worked hard to **accept** other people for who they are, **accepting** doesn't mean agreeing, necessarily. It means facing reality and seeking to understand it from a nonjudgmental standpoint. Understanding is a form of **acceptance**: understanding people, understanding situations, understanding how the universe works. It means knowing when something is over and walking away with dignity.

Being in a high-profile, very public relationship can be stressful. Your relationship is under a microscope in a sense. For a long time, my relationship with the ex-girlfriend people think my song is about was loving. We took care of each other. And I admired how hard she worked. She had goals and drive and was a very strong woman. But we were really young and not all that mature. We started to argue based on emotions and our egos as opposed to seeking out solutions. Sometimes we would take it too far and work to get the last word in or say things to hurt each other.

After doing couples therapy, we decided not to be together anymore. We had been through so much.

People think the song was a dis or a dig at her. Honestly, I didn't even write it with her in mind. I didn't want to hurt her. I was expressing myself and describing that feeling of moving on and feeling free. I actually wrote the song at a time when I wasn't going through any turmoil in my relationship. Everything was totally fine. It was just a concept that came to me and inspired me. After the relationship fell apart, I did end up changing one or two lines that expressed my current situation. I confess that could have been seen as petty, but I did it. But other than that, the song I released was pretty much how I wrote it while we were still together.

My experience with the song became very bittersweet, because I loved the success of it but I didn't like the narrative that it was unkind to her. I still cared for her as someone I'd shared love with for a long time. I felt bad sometimes, and I also felt a little defensive. There were things she was saying publicly about me at the time that hurt me, and so, when I saw people running with the narrative, I let it be. I'm not proud of how I handled that situation. I hoped that, as an artist herself, she'd understand that songs have a life of their own.

When I performed the song, I'd think it might be taking someone in the audience back to a moment in their life that they were glad was over. Maybe for them it was about an ex or their boss. Maybe they thought the song was kind of funny. Honestly, I didn't think about it too hard. I just enjoyed performing the song and seeing people's reactions.

But then something horrible and tragic happened years later: she died. She died while saving her son from drowning. And I was left with such confusing feelings of grief. I had moved on from our relationship. There was no interest there like that. But since we'd shared time and space together, it felt like a heavy loss. Her dying affected me profoundly. For quite some time, whenever I hopped in a pool, I thought of her trying to swim to safety. It made me feel sorry that I'd changed those lines and opened up the narrative that the song was about her and about revenge. Because the truth is, by the time she passed, we were cool.

A few months before the accident, I ran into her in a parking lot in Beverly Hills outside of a jazz club, and we had a friendly conversation. By this point, years and years had passed since the song was released. She had actually ended up performing it on a lip-sync TV show. I think she did that to show she didn't hold it against me anymore. She had also re-followed me on Instagram. So when we ran into each other, the feelings weren't that weird. She even said, "Hey, I want you to know it's all love." And we caught up for a couple of minutes.

We gave each other a hug and talked for a little while, and that was it. It was cool to see her and to make amends in real life. I loved that her life was going really well. It felt like we let go of anything damaging that had happened between us. It's always possible to make peace with someone and to let go of the hurt.

A few months after I saw her, I heard she'd been on a boat with her son, and while they were swimming in the water, she made a heroic effort to get him back in the boat when they got caught in a strong current. She was miraculously able to save him, but she couldn't get back on the boat herself. It is one of the most heroic and also devastating stories that I've ever heard. It affected me way more than I realized at first. When you've shared love with somebody, you're always going to have that between you, even if it changes form. I needed to **trust** in the truth of that.

Who do you need to make peace with?

Are you ready to let go of hurt
you've been holding on to?

When you free someone with forgiveness, you realize you were also a prisoner.

CHAPTER TWENTY

Forgiving Yourself

▪ *accepting*

EVERY SUNDAY, MY GRANDMA TOOK me to a nondenominational church called Unity. To be honest, I didn't love it. As a little kid, you have other stuff you'd rather do on the weekends. When I look back, though, I'm grateful for the structure and the ritual of it, and for how it helped teach me respect. I am a religious person and a very spiritual person, and I feel like it's good to hear a sermon. There's always something in it that applies to you. And those church days were all about family. We would have Sunday dinners together after church, and it was a cool time. It's funny how you don't really recognize a lot of blessings except in hindsight.

When I went to my grandma's house after school, she would have home-cooked food for us. I took it for granted and would often spoil my dinner on the way home by eating pizza or McDonald's. I regret that now. I should have been more respectful and grateful, especially because, when my grandmother had her stroke, it meant I'd never have her cooking again.

That's one of my biggest lessons I want to apply to myself today, to recognize the blessings I currently have so I can enjoy them now and not just when they're over. I tell myself, "Don't wait for people to die to let them know how you feel about them or to enjoy them." I also make sure to let go of the guilt I have around things I can no longer control.

A former employee of mine was at odds with her brother, and he ended up getting murdered. Her biggest regret in life was that he died before they could reconcile. Sometimes it takes something very big to show you how small all our problems really are.

I believe in identifying—either by journaling, in therapy, through meditating, or by talking to friends—what you're holding shame around. Then it's key to take the time to talk through it with yourself until you are reconciled to the fact that you're a human being and you're going to make mistakes. It took me a lot of therapy and a lot of time, but I finally got there, and I can tell you that life is better on the other side of that process.

Forgiving yourself—saying it and meaning it and feeling those feelings—can take some time. It might get a little emotional. That's okay! Forgiving ourselves is part of the work of **acceptance**. Letting go of how you think things should have been and seeing them for what they are is a gift to yourself. That also means you need to **accept** the unknown. **Accept** that it's going to work out for you and know that it's not all going to necessarily be clear in the moment.

We need to find forgiveness in all areas of life. You have to start by forgiving your people. Growing up, I used to look at my parents and older people like they were saints, like they could do no wrong, but my parents were just kids having kids, figuring it out. They were human and made some mistakes. That's something I had to realize over time.

Whether you need to forgive others or yourself, forgiveness is one of the most powerful gifts. I've known folks whose mothers died in childbirth, who grew up bearing the weight of feeling responsible for their mothers' death. We carry things with us that we can't possibly hold on to. Carrying the weight of guilt can destroy your energy frequency and hold you back in all kinds of ways without your even knowing. That's why, in seeking the progression of yourself, it's important to forgive anything that affects you or weighs you down, even if you think it doesn't matter. Many of us feel stuck because we haven't forgiven ourselves or forgiven others who've hurt us.

We should use forgiveness as a tool for freedom. We need to develop the self-awareness that what other people do (or don't do) is a reflection of what they are going through or a result of trauma from what they went through and what's been passed down to them. Finding forgiveness is one of the most crucial ways to understand how we exist together in one collective consciousness, and it's one of the most powerful things you can do to move higher on your own journey. When you are no longer held back by bearing unnecessary weight, you can fly.

What is your source of shame or regret? How could you use the practices in this book to help you let those feelings go?

Regret is the worst roommate.

CHAPTER TWENTY-ONE

Apologizing the Right Way

▪ *accepting, strategizing, trying, trusting*

RECENTLY, I WAS IN A situation in which I got into an argument, and the next day that person apologized to me, but the apology didn't come with any promise that there'd be an effort to change going forward. And so it didn't really work. The argument continued for a long time because there was no real resolution.

A therapist once told me that if you have an apology without a solution, then it's an empty apology. It's easy to say you're sorry. It's much harder to say that and then fully understand why there was a problem, and harder still to then **strategize** a solution and do something real about it, especially when you have to rewire yourself with new ways of thinking after doing something one way your entire life. The point of knowing better is to do better. Similarly, you might understand some of what I'm saying in this book, but if you don't apply it to your life, it's likely you won't remember it for long and it won't be as meaningful.

I have apologized in my life for things without giving a solution, and now, in hindsight, I realize that the apology wasn't complete. When I was a little kid, I used to steal $20 bills out of my grandma's drawer. It was very bad of me, and I did it a lot. Later on in life, I did confess and apologize for it. But my apology didn't come with a solution. I guess you could say stopping doing it was a solution, but the apology really should have come with a stack of twenty-dollar bills. I realized that I mostly apologized to make myself feel better.

I did end up buying my grandma and mama a house, but the two things don't really have anything to do with each other. If I'd never stolen the money, I still would've bought them that house.

People in relationships often wind up tying one thing to another when they don't have anything to do with each other. Just because I paid for your movie and popcorn doesn't mean that you have to pay for my dinner. Sometimes we hold stuff over people's heads and keep tabs on every exchange, when it's so much more fun and generative to do each other favors with no strings attached. Going tit-for-tat will cause conflict, confusion, and damage between people.

There have been situations in my life when someone's held favors they've done for me over my head, even if those favors weren't things I wanted. When you become a parent, there's so much to do. The challenge becomes about giving what you can at the time. It's usually not going to be exactly fifty-fifty. Sometimes it's eighty-twenty for a while, and then it switches to thirty-seventy. Keeping score can become damaging and detrimental to your relationship.

There are so many ways you could justify so many things. You could look in the Bible and you could justify killing a person, and you could also justify never harming anyone. I think that's why people have so much conflict in the world—they're so set on being right or proving that others are wrong.

A few years ago, I ran into a situation like this in my professional life, too. It's a long story, but basically I had a disagreement with a label over money. I said something about it in public because there was no movement toward resolution. There was pushback. Some people said, "Well, the fact that they gave you an opportunity and signed you is already a lot!" But that wasn't the agreement. Those things have nothing to do with each other.

Eventually, I worked my way out of that deal, but while I was under it, I sold more than a hundred million records.

Of course, I appreciate having been given the opportunity. But there has to be a break in the cycle of people constantly owing one another things.

I forgave myself for getting into that situation and for speaking out about it. Ultimately, I believe that we all make the decisions that we make; we just need to face the consequences associated with them, whatever they are, in the most straightforward and solutions-oriented way possible.

Regret is the worst roommate. You've got to live your life. **Trust** that it's all going to work out and that whatever you did isn't forever. You're a human being, and you can release a sense of guilt. Then when someone apologizes in a real way to you, you can offer them that same gift. You can work with them on the solution and refuse to let either of you dwell on it any longer.

Think of someone you feel like you owe an apology; then come up with a way to apologize with a solution.

Being in a relationship that doesn't serve you is like working the job you hate the most . . . for free.

CHAPTER TWENTY-TWO
Setting Boundaries

■ *strategizing, manifesting*

THE MOST POWERFUL LESSON I ever got in setting boundaries came from one of my best friends from high school. He was around when I was coming up, and he wanted to be a rapper as well. He was talented. So when my career started taking off, it was important to me to honor our relationship and share my platform with him the best I could.

There's an expectation (or unspoken rule) with rappers that you have to put your crew on your songs. I was doing my best to stick to that because that's what I was taught in the culture of rap, that you put your crew on after you get on.

This friend of mine was in the studio with me on the song "I Don't Fuck with You" and he came up with a line: "I just dodged a bullet from a crazy bitch."

I came up with the rest of the song, including the hook. So we're talking about one line out of seventy lines or so. The usual thing would have been to give him a little credit and a small writing fee. But I was looking out for him, so I offered him a little bit of money and also a percentage of the song. Then I invited him to be on another song on the same album with his favorite rapper ever, Lil Wayne.

But when it came time to work out the split of the publishing rights, he demanded what I thought was an outrageous percentage. In hindsight, I believe he was getting bad advice from people in his ear.

I told him, "Bro, this big a percentage is not realistic."

He held his ground. It held the song up in legal, causing me to miss an opportunity to get the song placed in a film, which ultimately cost me a lot of money. By the time the legal stuff was settled, it was too late to get it in the movie. It was a completely lost opportunity.

We're cool with each other now. We can still be friends. But when it comes to business, I have certain boundaries now. That was a very important lesson for me to learn.

Forgiveness is an inherent good. It allows you to let go of something negative you've been holding on to. Forgiveness is for the person who's forgiving, not only the person being forgiven. But here's the new lesson I've learned: establishing your boundaries is a very important part as well. Boundaries allow you to forgive more freely, knowing that you're not allowing someone negative back into your life in the same way just because you're offering them forgiveness.

Learning this lesson has been so valuable. When you choose to set boundaries, you gain so much power from deciding what you will allow to affect you. Detaching from a relationship that isn't serving you can be one of the most powerful things you can do for yourself. It's having the emotional intelligence to understand that how someone reacts to you is only a reflection of themselves.

For a long time, I knew how important it was to forgive someone. But I didn't realize that I had the wrong perception of forgiveness. I thought that when you forgave someone, it was supposed to be a reset and you had to go back to how things were. What I hadn't yet discovered is that you can forgive someone for past harm but still have your boundaries. Just because you don't have animosity and anger toward someone anymore doesn't mean you have to hang out with them. Ignoring warning signs about someone is self-sabotage. When you know the stove is hot but you still touch it, it's on you for getting burned.

Take a moment to recognize the other person's point of view, to have empathy. Realize that we are all on our own journey to figure ourselves out. Just because you forgive them doesn't mean you have to still be around them.

Recently, I've started to think about my song "I Don't Fuck with You" in a new way. I've come to realize that the "you" that you don't fuck with may be someone who's no longer helping you grow, or it may be a former version of yourself that you've outgrown. When I perform the song now, I feel joy, and I'm happy about the relief it may bring somebody by screaming and by saying goodbye to something that doesn't serve them anymore, whatever that may be.

You should always be growing, but you don't have to outgrow parts of yourself that are the best parts, the parts that bring you joy. In fact, I feel like one of the things I was sorry to outgrow was always having fun in everything I do. When I was a kid, I used to just have fun. Over time, that went away, and now I'm fighting to get it back. I feel like having fun, whatever you're doing, is the most important ingredient for success. You get what you give. If you're giving out fun, that's going to come back to you. Being stressed out in the world only makes more stress in the world, and that comes back on you, too.

I feel like everything I do is progress. And yet you don't want to outgrow every aspect of yourself. You only want to outgrow the aspects that don't align with who you are and that no longer serve you. Even though you are one person, there are so many different parts of you. And it's beautiful to keep growing. There's nothing to be ashamed of. It's actually something to celebrate. You might be mad at yourself for outgrowing something, and there are a lot of ways that growing can be painful. But it's important to **accept** your growth—you're maturing and changing, and that's okay! It's okay if something that you thought was supposed to happen didn't. It's okay to outgrow that and grow into something else.

Something I feel really good about having outgrown is a lax attitude toward my health, not understanding that I needed to take care of myself. I used to not eat the best that I could. I would get high and drink. I didn't have the foresight I do now. I've grown into thinking about myself a little more consciously, realizing that I'm demanding so much output from my body, and so I have to be conscious of what I'm putting into it—and not just food but in every aspect: mentally, physically, and emotionally.

Saying goodbye to people isn't necessarily sad. You may find that, as you do the internal work and continue to grow yourself, you've outgrown certain people, friends, or relationships. This is okay and natural. It's vital to set boundaries that protect your energy. Once you can understand someone and stop letting them affect you, no matter how much they bug you, have disrespected you, or are harmful to you in some other way, that's when you'll find peace.

Setting Boundaries

I've had to put up boundaries so that I wouldn't have people around in my life any longer in the same way. I had to rely on my own instincts. And I had to **manifest** a new reality in which those people would go off and be fruitful on their own. I could wish them nothing but the best fortune, but I would do it from a distance.

What boundaries would be useful to you going forward?

Success is something I hope we all get acquainted with. The only thing is, would you even recognize it when you come face-to-face with it?

CHAPTER TWENTY-THREE

Your Own Definition of Success

▪ *trusting*

I PERFORMED A SHOW IN Las Vegas recently, and I flew there and back with my DJ. He lives in Detroit now. He used to live in LA, but he moved back to where we grew up. I remember when he was first moving back, he was doing it because LA was too expensive for him. He said, "Man, I don't like living paycheck to paycheck. I have nothing to save after doing all these shows. It's not making sense to me."

He was so distraught at the idea of moving back to Detroit. He'd decided in his head that it was a defeat for him to move back. He had failed at something, at his job. I understood the feeling.

I love going back to my old neighborhood. It's just so much love, and it's a pleasure to be there. I love kicking it, sitting on a porch. I know the owners of the house that I grew up in. And I love that I got the key to the city one time, and that there's a Big Sean Day there, June 29. As much as I love my old neighborhood, though, I wanted to get up out of there, to live in other places, experience the world.

So I got it when my friend was sad to move back. That was in February 2020, and he got his situation together, but he was still having a tough time. When the pandemic hit, he said, "Wow. I didn't realize what a good idea it was that I moved back to Detroit. I wouldn't have been able to function or survive financially if I'd been out in LA for the pandemic. Because I moved back to Detroit, all these beautiful opportunities arose for me to make so much money."

He started booking Tigers and Pistons games, all because of the reputation that we had built together in the city and the reputation that he'd built on his own for being a quality, go-to DJ for big events. He's done almost everything a DJ can do when it comes to touring. He's played stadiums and arenas, small crowds and big crowds, plus everything in between. He said to me, "I've bought a couple of houses now. I'm selling my old house. I'm stacking this money. Man, I don't even want to live in LA now. I have the means to, but I don't even want to because it doesn't fit right."

All I could think was, look how God was working in your favor and you didn't even know because you had these previous expectations that might not have been useful to you. Perhaps they were somebody else's standards and not relevant to your life. A lot of us are working too hard to live by other people's ideas of what we should be doing.

In addition to the daily challenges that we all face, there's also an imagined race that we put ourselves in when it comes to life and deadlines, these expectations that we put on ourselves or that we feel we have to meet. We might feel that if we don't, we can't achieve happiness. The truth is that those fantasies about what success might look like often don't correspond with what we need on a deeper level.

Sometimes we give other people too much power. Some people get so upset if they are told by someone else that they've made something that's not good. But if you're the one who created it, why do you feel like someone critiquing it is that big a deal? That's something that I struggle with as an artist, too. We give so much power to these critics. But when we're the main ones creating something, who gives them the right to say if it's good or bad?

It's important to create your own definition of success and to understand that it looks different for everybody. You can't waste time comparing your life to someone else's, because we are all on our own unique journeys. There is no "failing" as long as you're following your intuition, even if you aren't meeting a goal that you set for yourself. What is it about the people you look up to that inspires you? Know that there is a difference between comparing yourself to them and being inspired by them. No one knows it all. We're all students of life, no matter how young, old, experienced, educated, or accomplished we are.

One of the most powerful things you can do to change your life is to be open to new pathways and possibilities and the myriad places from which those can emerge. Keep an open mind and approach life as a student, constantly learning (and unlearning) things in order to become the most elevated version of yourself. If you're following your heart and staying true to yourself, you're winning already. Everything else is the sprinkles on top. It's important to become conscious of your feelings and your thoughts, and to always remember that what you put out you will get back.

Negative self-talk is toxic, and it's pervasive. We create "standards" based on the things we think we need to achieve, largely due to societal expectations, and then beat ourselves up when we don't meet the societal standards that we bought into.

A lot of us are living in pursuit of an invented idea of success or even a previous idea of success that no longer applies. It's something to recognize and to be aware of, because releasing yourself from these expectations will save you a lot of pain and despair and depression or anxiety and help you live a happier life.

A righteous person has his heart in the right place at all times. And when you're like that, the universe is working with you, whether you know it or not, even if sometimes it takes a while to see. We have to do the self-work to have the clear sight and humility to be in a place to receive the gifts the universe wants to give us.

One of my heroes in learning how to define success on your own terms is my older brother, Brett. It can be hard for a man's ego to have a younger brother who becomes a rap star and starts making money. But Brett has never once showed an ounce of jealousy or resentment. He's always supported me fully and barely ever asked me for anything. He never hits me up for money unless it's an absolute last resort, and usually only for something thoughtful he wants to do for our mom that he'd like me to chip in on.

Recently, he's been staying with me, spending time with me and seeing Noah. He can stay as long as he wants, because I feel like I have a lot to learn from him. He's a very smart person and reads more than anyone I know, something like thirty books last year. He's definitely someone who I feel never judges me. I really love my brother, and I admire how he sets his own goals, whether in the gym when we work out together or in his work as a day trader. He finds ways to push himself enough to feel motivated but not so hard that he doesn't enjoy his life. I hope to be more like him. Sometimes I fall victim to not always seeing the invisible race I'm running, and I don't recognize my salvation when it's right in front of me.

My mother always likes to tell the parable of the two boats and the helicopter. It's been around at least since the 1980s; you may have seen it used as a title in the HBO show *The Leftovers*. A man is on his roof, and the floodwaters are rising. He prays for God to save him. A rowboat comes by. The rescuer says, "Get in!" And he says, "No, God's going to save me." A motorboat comes by. He says, "No, God's going to save me." Then a helicopter throws down a rope ladder. He says, "No, God's going to save me."

He dies. When he gets to heaven he says, "You were supposed to save me!" And God says, "I sent you two boats and a helicopter!"

Sometimes the answers we're looking for are right in our face, and we're so blinded by our expectations and our beliefs that we don't even see our salvation. We need to **trust** that the universe is going to find a way to take care of us, and we need to do our best to see what that is.

Are there ways you could be blocking your own success? Is not having the proper mindset or having a negative outlook or a belief about how things should go as opposed to letting the universe guide you stopping you from becoming your highest self?

God doesn't always give you what you want; God gives you what you need.

CHAPTER TWENTY-FOUR
Making Room

▪ *accepting, trusting*

LIFE GIVES YOU THINGS THAT you don't know you need. That's how I felt about the fact that my mom came and stayed with me during the pandemic, a situation that I had to **accept** and that I couldn't change. Not what I wanted, but God doesn't always give you what you want; God gives you what you need.

The depression I dealt with after getting off Adderall took a toll on my relationship with my mom. I didn't call and check up on her often, and when I did, we barely talked. I felt ashamed of myself and my life. My estrangement from her was part of a bigger problem with how I was seeing myself: I felt like I didn't deserve to have a relationship with my family. I felt like I didn't deserve to go out to clubs and party. I'd built this false narrative up in my brain that my family's love was conditional, and so they wouldn't love me anymore once I was no longer happy and fun.

As my brain was rewiring and I was starting to work on myself, my mom wanted to come visit me in October 2019, and she wanted to stay the whole winter to get a series of IV treatments from a holistic doctor here in LA. I had a house in Beverly Hills, and there was plenty of room.

She arrived. Time passed. We got along well, though I started to think maybe it would be nice to live alone again. Then she said, "If it's okay with you, I'll just go back to Detroit after your birthday in March."

I love my mom, so I said, "Great," even though I thought that was way too long.

Then the beginning of March came, the pandemic happened, and she had to stay put. Everyone was thinking that it was only going to last a month or two. A year went by with my mom still in my house.

Finally, people were starting to travel again. I asked her if she had thought about going home. I could tell she was a little hurt. The next day she told me that she was leaving in a couple of days. I told her that I didn't want her to leave that soon, but she said, "No, I already booked my way back home. Plus they upgraded the plane, so I want to take advantage of that."

"I didn't know that Delta tells you when they upgrade the plane," I said.

"Oh, I didn't book Delta," she said. "I booked a private flight."

I figured I'd be paying for that. *Hmm*, I thought. I don't even fly private myself; I fly commercial. *She must be mad*.

When the day came, I drove her to her plane. As we headed to the airport, I realized that, in those months together, we'd had a lot of wonderful times. We'd gotten angry at each other plenty, but we'd also really been there for each other and had a closer relationship than we'd had since I was a kid.

I found myself feeling grateful that she was getting on a private plane all by herself because so many people were dying of Covid, including one of her best friends.

When it was time to say goodbye, she and I hugged. We both started crying in each other's arms.

"I'm so proud of the man you've become," she said. "You're such a good man."

It was a really emotional moment, and something that I don't think would have happened without all that time together, even if I hadn't exactly asked for it or thought it was what I needed.

Even if it's something that I didn't want, to spend a year and a half with my mom, when I look back on it, it probably helped reset a certain part of my life. One day she won't be here, and I'll always remember that time and how we became close again after being so far apart.

In the days after she left, I started walking around the house naked, just because I could. One day I just yelled these deafening therapeutic screams. If you yell at the top of your lungs in the house with someone else around, they'll worry about you. It felt good to be able to do that and not worry anyone. Because I was fine. It just felt good to have my space back. But I was still really glad that I restored my relationship with my mom. In the house in Michigan where she lives, I keep a room for myself in the basement.

One of the songs I wrote for my mom that still makes her cry is "Inspire Me." I don't always answer her phone calls. I don't necessarily want her living with me full-time. But she's so important to me. She's the first person that I rapped for, and she supports me like nobody else does.

What or who have you had
to make space for?

What's one thing you
thought was a sacrifice that
turned out to be a gift?

Remember the five Ps: Proper Preparation Prevents Poor Performance. The thing is, though, you just can't prepare for every stage of life.

CHAPTER TWENTY-FIVE

Discomfort Can Be Good

▪ *accepting, trying, trusting, manifesting*

AT THIS POINT, IT'S RARE that I get super-nervous before a show, but I was in a real state leading up to my 2022 Coachella show. I had never performed there. I was supposed to appear in 2020 and then in 2021, but both were canceled because of Covid. So, finally, I was going to be performing there, and on one of the biggest stages. Everyone was so excited for the act that was before me. There was a lot of buzz online about him, and I didn't know what that meant for my set.

I had on all white. As I walked through the dusty-ass festival grounds, I thought, *Man, what if everyone sees the other guy and then leaves before I go on?* Then I thought, *No, I have faith in myself.*

On my way there, I meditated, and I visualized things going well until I **accepted** that it was going to be an incredible show. All day and all night, I had been getting texts from people who were already there, saying, "Oh, man, the crowd here at Coachella is dry." All of these people who had all this buzz, all these big artists—word was, "Oh, it wasn't that good for them." I was watching clips and saying, "Oh, yeah, this doesn't look too good."

But, for some reason, I had visualized the crowd and seen them 100 percent locked in with me. I saw it being one of the best shows of my life, and I **accepted** that. So when I opened my eyes, even though I saw the person performing before me speed past in a golf cart while I was walking through the dirt, I held my head high and **trusted** that it was going to be an amazing show.

Throughout my life, I've felt uncomfortable whenever I'm facing something new, from the first day of school to the first time I wrote a rap. From the first time I met Kanye and freestyled for him at the radio station to the first time I was in a studio with him or with Eminem. Early on in my career, and even now sometimes, I felt uncomfortable. But through this inner work, I've been able to shift my perspective on that feeling. Feeling uncomfortable signals to me that I'm about to encounter an opportunity to learn or grow.

When I'm working out, I feel uncomfortable. I'm pushing myself out of my comfort zone as much as I can because that's where the growth is. Working out is the simplest form of that because you see the results. It's something that, on a very surface level, follows this simple equation: you put more work in, you see more results. Muscle is built by literally tearing the existing muscle apart. Success is like that. It's not just for your body or your career; it's true of everything. Success can mean reaching whatever goal you set, whether that's raising a polite child or getting a good job or just getting out of bed in the morning.

For me that day, my goal was to do a truly great show. So I got there, and when I got to my trailer, my partner and collaborator, Jhené, was there. She was pregnant with Noah at the time. No one knew. She was only about two and a half months along. She said, "Hey, it's going to be great." She was very encouraging, and everyone around me was, too. Then the guy went on before me, and he completely murdered it. I heard the crowd.

I thought, *Wow, they were turned up for him. Oh, man, I hope they're turned up for me. But I wouldn't be here if I wasn't meant to be here. And if I'm meant to be here right now, then this is going to go well.*

I was so ready to go in that minute, so *on*, that whether the crowd was there or not, whether the praise came or not, I still would've put on one of the best shows of my life.

Right before I got on stage, there were a couple of fans on the side of the stage, and they were like, "We've been waiting for you all day. We love you." That made me feel great. Harry Styles and I were on at the same time, and I heard that the crowd was evenly split between us.

It was a great show, and it was big, big, big. I remember thinking to myself, *I'm done ever questioning my faith again*. And I thought all of this happened because I lived my practices: **accepting** that whatever happened was happening for a reason, **trying** my hardest, and **manifesting** the best version of myself.

The number of people isn't necessarily a sign of how well it went. It was the feeling that I got on stage. I was in my flow, in my moment.

Some people say I'm an overthinker. But I would say I'm a thorough thinker. One of the hardest lessons I've had to learn is that whenever you're **trying** to excel in something, whatever profession you're in, it's okay to be uncomfortable.

In fact, I think I prefer having that sense of discomfort now because I know it means I'm in uncharted territory, which means that

I'm doing something I'm not used to, and that has endless possibilities on every level. You may be coming up with something that will inspire a whole generation, so learn to embrace being uncomfortable. If you can embrace being uncomfortable, then there's nothing that life can throw at you to bring you down—not for long, at least.

You've got to remember that, no matter what happens, there's always an opportunity in life. If you're at the top of your game in whatever it is you do, you have an opportunity. If you completely bomb and you're at the bottom, you have an opportunity there, too. You have to recognize every aspect, every situation as the opportunity, and you have to seize the opportunity, whatever it has to teach you.

When in your life have you felt uncomfortable? Can you look back on that time now and see what opportunity appeared as a result?

Is there a time in your life when what you were afraid of happened to you and you survived it? What were you so afraid of?

I always remember when it comes to other people: *These are this person's feelings; I don't have to take them on as mine.*

CHAPTER TWENTY-SIX

Letting Go

▪ *accepting, trying*

ONE THING I'M LEARNING AS a new father is that you can't protect your child from everything. But one of the things that I can do is teach him. In turn, Noah teaches me. I learn from my son every day I'm with him, whether it's to have more patience or to appreciate the simple things when we're on our walks.

There are times when he reaches delicately for a flower and I marvel at how he's able to know that, if he grabbed it, he would destroy it. It's been therapeutic for me. Sometimes I get caught up in my career, and then I realize Noah needs my attention. Suddenly everything I was fretting about seems unimportant next to him. Carrying him around is a physical workout for me, too. By the end of a long walk with him in my arms, wriggling around, I'm pouring sweat!

Of course, I want to protect him. I don't want him to bump his head, but guess what? Sometimes he bumps his head. There are times when I'm watching him closely and he's doing well moving around, and then, out of nowhere, he'll hit his head on something and start crying. I rock him and kiss him and say, "Oh my God, bro! Why did you do that?"

Sometimes children have to go through things. But as far as teaching my son, I want to teach him early on to **accept** and love whatever it is he's passionate about in the world. As long as he has the right intentions behind it and a good heart, I know that he'll be fine. I know that he'll have a lovely life and he'll go through his ups and downs; he'll go through his hardships and his own trauma, but I hope that he attracts the people that he needs in his life and that he learns from and gets inspiration from the right mentors. I pray for him to have a life where he learns a lot and develops a lot and progresses and carries on the best of me and his mom.

Even though I want him to succeed, I find that, deep down, I'm not worried about him. He's so bright and beautiful and smart. He catches on so fast. I think he's going to be fine with the right guidance and love. I worry that if we hyper-manage our kids, we could be robbing them of the greatest gift that they have, which is their limitless imagination.

When I do my affirmations while holding him, he's often very still. He usually sits in my arms facing the world, not facing me. I hold him so that he sits up above in front of my chest, and I'm holding his legs and his torso.

Sometimes he laughs and giggles. Sometimes he's completely silent with his eyes open, watching the world. He's a very expressive baby, especially when we're outside. He loves being outside. He definitely has some type of Buddha energy going on because he is so in tune with nature, and when he sees a picture of Buddha or a Buddha statue, he sometimes starts smiling and wants to touch it.

There's no doubt about it. He's an old soul, and he appreciates the essence of nature and the world. The other day, we got close to a beautiful butterfly. The butterfly let him touch it—the gentlest whisper of a touch of his baby finger on the butterfly's wing—and then the butterfly flew away. I was very surprised and impressed with how gracefully he did that. Then there are times when he grabs the dog hard, so he's still learning his control, his own strength.

He's getting more curious, more energetic, more active. He always does things his own way. He has a unique kind of crawl, sort of a scoot. I'm letting him be who he is and encouraging it.

I always remember when it comes to other people: *These are this person's feelings; I don't have to take them on as mine.* I even have to remember that with my son. There are times when he can have a strong effect on my emotional state. Lately, he's been coughing, and it bothers me so much. As a new father, I was distraught the first time he coughed. I wanted to take him to the hospital. But after he coughs, he laughs and smiles. It's not an emergency. I have to tell myself, *Okay, when your immune system is developing, it's fighting off germs, and that's all coughing or a runny nose is.*

When I look at it from that positive perspective, I can see it not as *Oh no! He's sick!* but as *My son is getting stronger. His immune system is fighting something, and he's going to come out the other end of the cold with his immune system even more developed.* And looking at it like that takes that worry away. His body is protecting him. His mother and I are protecting him as much as we can—especially his mother. She is really on it. And when I do my meditations, I wrap him in all the other protections I can summon.

I see him finding his own teachers in addition to his family. He loves Ms. Rachel. She's the new phenom for babies. She started making videos for her daughter, who had a speech impediment, when she noticed the lack of content for kids with speech problems. And then she started uploading her videos for other kids. That touched me, because my dad had a speech impediment, and I always wondered where it came from and how someone might have helped him with it when he was growing up.

Ms. Rachel's videos have hundreds of millions of views now. I'm happy to see that one of Noah's first teachers is joyful and fun, and there to help him communicate better. May he have many, many more teachers in his life like that. And may I never forget that learning something new, **trying** new things, is the best way to set yourself on a new path or bring yourself back to your passion. And there's nothing more fun than introducing Noah to new things, whether that's new foods or his first time at the zoo.

Throughout Noah's life, I hope he will have teachers who value kindness and have a true love of life. And I expect that, for his whole life, I'll wrestle with questions about wanting to protect him, while knowing that he needs to experience challenges to grow and prosper. For now, I will just love learning, along with him, about the wonders of the universe.

What are you trying to control right now that you could let go of?

What lessons might you learn if you slowed down and took a beat?

I need to stop acting like life will always be waiting on me to live it. Now is the time!

CHAPTER TWENTY-SEVEN

Taking the Time It Takes

▪ *accepting, trying*

ON NEW YEAR'S 2020, I saw Kobe Bryant at a party. Kobe and I got to talking. Obviously, he was one of my all-time favorite basketball players. He also attributed a lot of his precision to daily meditation. We exchanged phone numbers, and he told me to text him. I said, "I appreciate it. I'd love to get with you sometime." He told me he'd love to hear my new music. I was excited for him to hear it, but I put off reaching out to him because I was still fine-tuning it. It had been mostly ready; I just figured I had plenty of time to get it right before I invited him over. Less than a month later, Kobe was killed in a tragic helicopter crash. I know I'm not alone in strongly feeling that loss.

If I've learned anything in my lifetime, it's that we are here for a limited time only. We need to take advantage of the time we have; you can't expect someone to always be there. None of us knows when our expiration date will be. It's easy to feel fear when you realize how short life is and understand your mortality, but I believe in the power of embracing that fear and using it as motivation. One of my favorite questions to ask people, and myself, too, is, "What are you going to do with the time you've got left?"

There are so many people who are paralyzed by fear and do nothing, or who pay so much attention to what other people are doing that they're distracted from working on their own sense of self-acceptance.

We need to treat our short lives with appreciation and recognition of how precious each moment is. We are leasing these bodies. They will break down. I don't mean you have to quit your job and travel the world. I mean do what you need to do to create a life you love. Treat people with grace and kindness. Acknowledge everyone as a human being. And when you figure out your purpose in life, you can't waste any time in getting started. It's not depressing—it's motivating. Whatever that is for you, go after it, and treat every day with the reverence it deserves.

You can't fully understand what it means to live your life to the fullest and to reach your highest potential until you've done the work of self-understanding. Whether you're working on understanding your own life experiences or realizing how you fit into the larger social ecosystem, we can all understand how precious life is when we experience loss. That loss can remind us how important our relationships are and how blessed we are to have those relationships, and it can inspire us to work harder to appreciate life every day.

First and foremost, there's no wrong way to spend your time. There are times when I have so much to do, so much that I'm supposed to do, but I feel like lying down and watching TV. I'm tired. There have been times when I've also felt like I didn't deserve to relax because the job wasn't done. I don't know where I inherited this mindset from.

I'd hear, "Yo, we should go out to dinner tonight and have a good time, link with friends." I would feel guilty doing that because I felt I had work to do. Now I see that that is such a backward way of thinking. A good time with friends can never be a waste.

For a long time, I didn't realize how important it is to enjoy your life. I think doing so comes with **accepting** God's timing.

Here's an example I'm going through now. As I'm writing this book, I'm also working on my album. It's sounding amazing so far. But things are taking longer than I would like because I have teams that are working on my merchandise, teams that are working on editing music videos, and teams that are editing pictures from the photoshoots. All these things are happening simultaneously but are also intertwined.

I heard myself saying, "Guys, I need it out now. I need it out now because I want to have my album done before the Grammy cutoff!" I have loved being nominated for Grammys. I always figured that, when you work hard, it's nice to have someone acknowledge it.

My label agreed with me. They said, "We're rushing to get it out!"

But then I had to think about whether everything was truly ready. I had to ask myself, "Do I want to rush if it will be bad for the work? Am I putting out something that my ego is telling me is important over God's timing for the work?"

I had to focus on what was best for my music and what the universe had in store for it, not some arbitrary timeline that I was imposing on it to feed my ego.

When I race through recording, it doesn't feel natural. It's like I'm pushing it. It's good to push it some, to let the universe know you desire something. But there's also striking a balance in order to preserve the quality of the work. I think you have to know the line between pushing for something and hustling and sprinting toward a goal; to know when you're forcing something. It's a thin line sometimes.

I'm learning to relax more, to say, "Hey, man, whatever's meant to be will be—and whatever isn't won't. It's okay; enjoy it." Because when you're enjoying something and you put joy into it, I feel like that's when the magic comes.

You have to be aware enough that when you're in these moments, you're able to think and **accept** and understand and apply everything you've learned in real time. When you look back on a situation, you can always say, "Oh, I should have done that differently. Oh, I could have done this, I should've done that," but it takes mastery for you to be aware of how to use these lessons and to still be joyful through it all. That's something that I have to actively remind myself to do.

I **accept** that I won't always do everything perfectly. For instance, sometimes there have been songs that didn't completely work out. I always learn through trial and error what works and what doesn't work. And I choose to see it that way, regardless of the degree of commercial success.

We change, and doing the same exact thing doesn't always work. You have to treat every song, every situation, differently. For me, every album, every performance, every interview, every meeting, every teammate, every employee—it all changes over time. And you have to honor that and always **strategize** based on the new reality. It's unlikely that you'll ever be 100 percent satisfied with where you are. But when you're doing your best all the time, eventually things work out for the best.

The phrase "next year" doesn't scare me like it used to. I feel grateful to have another year to **try** to make a difference, to make music I believe in, to be there for my family. But I do feel time is going very fast. That's why it's important to slow things down as much as I can. My concept of time has changed dramatically.

Before, it used to be stressful. I would be on the set of a video and have people run up to me, saying, "Did you listen to the master of this song? Did you approve that?" And I'd have a thousand things in my head right as I was going out to perform in front of a camera for something that was about to be immortalized. That pressure sucked the fun out of everything. When you stack up too many things, you're not present for any of them.

I've since learned that there are two kinds of stress: eustress, which exists for a period of time, feels good, and helps you hustle; and distress, which can last a long time and feels terrible. One causes excitement; the other causes anxiety. It can be hard to tell which one you're experiencing at any given time because they have a lot in common—a jacked-up kind of feeling that pushes you to do more. But one is constructive, and the other is destructive.

Time is relentless. It doesn't slow down for you unless you make it slow down. You've got to learn to either get with it or move on your own timing. There are no other options. You never know what day will be your last.

Nipsey Hussle was a good friend and an amazing artist. He worked so hard. Anybody who ever met him knew that he had vision and an incredible work ethic. He was working on *Victory Lap* for years. People were looking at him, saying, "When are you going to drop that already? Bro, you've been working on that for seven years!" But he was right. That album is a true classic. That gave me the confidence to stand my ground whenever I've been pressured to be done with something before I think it's ready. I have to stick to my guns. That's something Nip did his whole career. He's a legend to me for that.

In early 2019, Nipsey invited me to his video shoot. The shoot was far away, and I started doing the calculations in my brain of what time I would get there, how long it would take, and what would be happening by the time I got there; ultimately, I decided to tell him, "Damn, I'm not gonna make it." Nipsey and I had recorded a song together for my next album, but I'd procrastinated finishing it because, for whatever reason, I couldn't find the inspiration to figure it out all the way.

Then on March 31, 2019, Nipsey was shot and killed. Sometimes, in the studio, I hear something and think, "Nip wouldn't have gone with that," and I change it.

I'm hopefully only about a third of the way through my life. I've seen so much, but I have a lot more I want to accomplish. What I've learned is that when I was rushing to get from one thing to the other, time started going way too fast. Ironically, the only way to make time feel like it's stretching out is to slow down and fully appreciate every minute.

What is taking longer than you'd like? Can you visualize that thing happening on God's time, not yours? Close your eyes and visualize the thing you want to happen actually happening. Imagine it happening tomorrow, next year, in ten years. Make peace with every one of those timelines. Let go of your need to control the timing.

I've been listening to
my heart . . . on repeat.

CHAPTER TWENTY-EIGHT

The Universe Has a Plan

▪ *trusting*

THE OTHER NIGHT I WAS in the studio at home working on a song, and all of a sudden, a police helicopter flew over my house, a searchlight beaming all around the neighborhood. I ran outside to find twenty cops there. I learned that three houses had been broken into. In my neighborhood, that's rare. My neighbors, who have lived here for thirty years, told me that kind of thing had never happened.

My house was burglarized years before when I was out of town, in Dubai with my family. I knew how violating it can feel. That time, we looked back at video footage and saw people with night-vision goggles who ran up and spray-painted the security cameras black. I didn't keep much money at home, but they got a lot of rare sneakers, like my Louis Vuitton Jaspers with the pink bottoms, which go for around $15,000.

This time my house didn't get hit, but a bunch of my neighbors' houses did. While I was standing there, taking in the scene, my new neighbor came out of his house across the street. He was a cool-looking guy with white hair, and he seemed not even remotely concerned.

After a second, I realized that he was James Gunn, who wrote and directed the *Guardians of the Galaxy* movies for Marvel Studios and who is the current head of DC Studios.

"Oh shit, what's up, man?" I said.

He recognized me, too, and said, "Oh, hey!"

I don't usually get too excited about meeting famous people, but this was different. I'm a huge nerd when it comes to comic books, anime, television shows, scripts, acting, and cinematography. I love all that stuff very, very much. And here was one of the kings of that world.

It turned out that he'd been my neighbor for a few months. Sadly, his house was one of the ones that was broken into.

I ended up giving him my number, and he texted me later on. We wrote back and forth for a while, and then he invited me over to smoke cigars with him and his homies. I went over and had such a great time talking about movies with all of them. We like a lot of the same things. It was a really cool experience.

His wife saw us talking and said, "Man, you guys were meant to meet!"

"Yeah," I said. "That's the universe, working in strange ways."

Friends of mine I told about this budding friendship got all excited and said, "Maybe he'll put you in a movie!"

I don't think that way. I don't expect anything to come out of a friendship. And working to get more from something that's already wonderful is being greedy. That connection was such a joy. It was a gift, being able to talk about stuff that I'm passionate about with somebody who's also passionate about it and about creating things.

I was thankful to the universe for this new friend I could talk to. If that was the only time we ever spent together, that would have been enough. Having no expectations is important. Sometimes expectations can ruin an experience for you. Life can also exceed your expectations.

The difference between an expectation and an intention is that an intention is something that is related to an openness to changing for the better. It's my intention to be a good friend to James Gunn, because I admire him and love talking with him about movies. That's what I intend to do. When you're expecting something instead—which might be thinking, as my friend suggested, "We're going to be best friends now, and he's going to give me a part in his next movie!"—that sets you up for failure on every level.

None of us is entitled to anything. We all have opportunities. Some of us start with advantages or disadvantages, or disadvantages that seem like advantages, or advantages that seem like disadvantages. Everyone's story is different. But no one has to give us anything, ever.

An intention with the right energy behind it, though, is meaningful. People can feel the difference.

If I had gone over the first time I met Jay-Z and expected to get a verse from him, he'd have been turned off, and I would've left feeling devastated. But that wasn't that case. Now, did I intend one day to make music with Jay-Z? Yeah, I *intended* to, but I didn't *expect* to. And then it did finally happen.

What's more, Jay-Z gave me the ultimate symbol of respect: a Roc-a-Fella chain. I mentioned how much I loved that piece, and next thing I know, he's texting me: "What size chain you want—mid- or full-size?"

What would you say? I said, "Full-size!"

Next thing I know, he's saying, "Go pick it up from the jeweler. You've earned it, man. I hope you wear it with pride."

Nothing happens purely by accident. Things are a culmination of moments that build up to now. Now I have a great relationship with Jay-Z, and his company manages me. He's an awesome person; I get to talk to him once in a while and have dinner with him or play new music for him and get his advice. He's very helpful. And it's cool because we both have the same first name, too (except he spells his wrong). We always have a great time when we talk.

The first time I met Jay-Z, I shook his hand and thought, *Man, I have got to work with him*. I had to figure out how I was going to make that happen, and it actually happened without my even asking. So that was beautiful. But that's the thing: In all the important aspects of your life, you don't really have to worry. You have to do the work, but you don't have to worry. You just have to put the vibes out there and put your best foot forward, **trusting** that one day you're going to get your shot.

It had always been a dream of mine to be on songs with Jay-Z and Eminem and Lil Wayne. Now, looking back, I'm happy I've had moments with them and so many people in music who I respect so much and grew up listening to. When I made a song in London while all of us at G.O.O.D. Music were cooking up something for a possible compilation, I came up with an idea for a song called "Clique." I was just making music, having fun, and expressing myself. I left it on the computer and thought nothing of it.

The next thing I know, a few weeks later, Jay-Z and Kanye and I are on the song. This was right after they did their *Watch the Throne* album. So for sure it was an awesome opportunity and something that I put out the intention of doing but didn't have any expectations about.

Originally, there were eight other people on the song. They took everyone off except me and Ye. I didn't know that he would hop on that song, either. I just did a verse and a hook to the beat without thinking about it. I was just catching a vibe. Then I left it and almost forgot about it. That song, "Clique," has gone multiplatinum now. It was all over the radio, and I actually got a chance to perform it with Jay-Z in North Carolina on stage when I was on tour down there.

It's just crazy how the universe works. When you perform with Jay-Z, a lot of people throw up a pyramid with their hands. When I did that, I realized that my mom was in the Delta sorority, and that's their sign. And I'm pretty sure that my ancestors worked to build the pyramids. On that night, my whole past and future seemed to come together onstage around that symbol.

My connection to Jay-Z and that song happened because I put the intention out there with love, not greed. With intention, you're allowing yourself to be willing to enjoy whatever good things may come your way, as opposed to an expectation, where you're locked in on that specific thing.

I'm a huge fan of so many people. When I meet them, I fan out in my own way, but I also remember to be myself and that they are people who are going through their lives as well. You never know what they're going through. That's why I always also hope to be supportive. I love genuinely complimenting someone when I get the chance or letting them know what impact their work has had on me.

I recently got another text from James Gunn. "Yo, I'm working on the new *Superman*. You should come down and be on the set with me. Check it out. I have the best sets in the game, man. You should come hang out."

Again, I was being given more than I asked for, and I think it was because I **trusted** the universe and had no expectations.

What is an intention you can set right now that you're hoping to fulfill?

What's something that you appreciate for what it is and not what it could do for you in the future?

What if this is our only time to progress ourselves on a spiritual level? When you realize how much information our DNA contains, you'll see that the answer you're searching for may already live within you.

CHAPTER TWENTY-NINE

The Soul's Progress

▪ *accepting, manifesting*

EVERY DAY OF MY LIFE, I feel the protection of my grandma, my granddad, and my ancestors. I really appreciate the protection of my angels. But I also want them to move on to the next part of their consciousness.

When I told this to my brother, Brett, he said, "I'm so glad you mentioned this. Spiritual energy is universal, not specific. Even when you're in your physical body, you never stop being a spiritual being. In your purely spiritual form of being, you could be multiple things at once, and time also isn't linear. So, in other words, Grandma's soul could be a baby right now somewhere, while she's also watching over you and doing something else all at the same time."

To me that makes total sense. I love talking to my brother about past and future lives, and I find that thinking about different forms of consciousness has real-world effects.

Not long after that conversation with Brett, I had bad throat problems. I didn't know if it was my thyroid. It felt like it was a big lump. It was sore, too, and really weird. I was getting concerned. It lasted for a couple of weeks.

I was traveling and doing a lot of work, under a lot of stress, which could have heavily contributed to it. It started to get better, but then it started hurting again when I was playing with Noah and again when I was falling asleep, just as bad as when it had first started hurting two weeks before.

I'm a person who meditates and prays all the time. But this was the first time that this experience had happened to me. So I went to sleep that night with my throat hurting, and I woke up and took a look at the clock, which read 5:36. Then I heard a voice. I know this sounds crazy, but I really believe that it was the voice of God or the universe or whatever you want to call it speaking to me. It was a voice that was both very familiar and something I'd never heard before.

The voice said, "If you don't use your voice, I can take it away."

I thought I was dreaming, but I wasn't. The voice said the same thing again, which was very clear. I got crazy goose bumps. I didn't take it as a threat, either. I didn't take it as "You better use your voice." I took it as "You've been blessed with your voice. If you don't want to use it, you don't have to have it." Simple as that. It was actually very loving.

As soon as I **accepted** this information, my throat started feeling 50 percent better. Immediately, there was a release, and I knew I needed to use my voice in all aspects of my life—in my music, in my work as an author, in my personal life, out in the world.

I needed to be more forthcoming about my feelings, and I needed to work harder not to be a people-pleaser. Fact is, I'm a very understanding person, so sometimes I don't really look at things as right or wrong. I always can see where someone is coming from. I'm naturally a nice guy. I'm empathetic, and I feel for the other person. But with that mindset, I never really speak up because I'm more of a listener. Lately, I've been feeling the need to speak up more.

I think the habit of not speaking up has turned into a bad habit, because even if I feel a certain way, I always consider where someone else might be, even though I'm going through my own stuff as well. But I realize now that I have to use my voice. So I've been practicing speaking up in situations, even if expressing how I feel makes me uncomfortable. I respect that people are going through different human experiences, so I've been taking this message from the spirit seriously. Only a few days after that, my throat cleared up completely.

After what happened with my throat, I went to see a doctor. I wanted to make sure that everything was okay, because having a sore throat for more than a few days is kind of weird, especially when it mysteriously goes away. They did some tests, and I told her about the dream I'd just had.

My doctor is also very spiritual, so it didn't surprise me that she was unfazed by the story of this voice coming to me.

In fact, she had an interesting question about it: "Was it between five and six in the morning when you heard that voice?"

"Whoa, it was," I said. "It was actually 5:36."

Then she got goose bumps.

She told me that was a sacred time when people have historically said that they have heard the voice of God. Between 5:00 and 6:00 a.m. is when people often get these messages.

My point is, we are all spiritual beings inside our human bodies. Some people believe that. Some people think we're just human, and then once we die, our lights cut off. I even used to think that myself until I felt the presence of my grandparents who had passed. It was then that I knew. There were also just certain omens and signs that there is something that happens after this, guaranteed for sure. It's not lights out to me.

It's just one concept, and it's not something I want to debate. I don't want people to say, "Oh, let me prove to you why that's wrong," because none of us really knows. But I had an idea that felt right to me, which is that if we are to **accept** that we are spiritual beings, souls that get poured into this body where we experience hurt, pleasure, pain, eating food, having sex, depression, anxiety, stress, happiness, and bliss—a whole range of different emotions—then when we leave our human body, emotions may not be needed anymore.

I was also thinking that if there aren't any of those challenges, then how much progression does the soul make after we leave our body? What if this is our opportunity to progress our souls, so that when we leave our body we are actually elevated and expanded?

That's another reason why it's so important to work on yourself. Obviously, it's very important to work on your goals and your career, all these amazing things and projects to leave behind for the next generation of your family. But it's also important to work on yourself in order to progress your soul. This may be the real reason that we are born—not just to progress the world but to progress ourselves and expand our soul with more knowledge and lessons.

I'm not hoping to prove anything. I'd just like to pose a "what if" question: What if this is our only time to progress ourselves on a spiritual level? While we're in a human body, what if it's our only time to grow in that way? How would you look at depression then? Would you think your problems would be vanquished through a desire to take your own life, or would you look at your struggle more as growing pains as you progress as a person, and actually one of the main reasons why you're on this planet?

When you look at life like that, it kind of makes it a little bit more bearable. It doesn't necessarily make it not true that I don't feel the emotion, but it makes me feel a little bit more like everything I'm doing is because I'm **trying** to expand. And I better do as much as I can now because, once I'm dead, I won't be able to do this work anymore.

Even with all that I do to stay grounded, I struggle to remember this when times are hard. While I was working on this book and making my new album, I got really sick. I think I get sick when life gets heavy, when I've got a lot of work, a lot of responsibility being a dad, a lot of traveling, and other things I'm **trying** to balance.

This time my body just made the decision for me to settle down and be still. When things like that happen, I always ask, *What is the universe telling me right now? What is God saying?* It's kind of like that thing where you get a warning, and you get another warning, and then it comes hard. It starts smacking you up against the head after a while.

I always make sure that I'm not missing the point, that I can stop the hustle for a second and see if there's a reason why something happened. I always at least hope to be conscious about what's going on and not look at things from a victim's mindset. Instead of thinking "Why me?" I come to it as someone who is more self-aware and conscious. I'm asking the same questions, but putting different energy behind it.

I feel like I'm in touch with my higher self when I'm open to that conversation: I've been told to rest, that I need to get organized, get clarity, and get focused. It's not always easy. While I'm resting, I look at the calendar, and I know I have a lot of things that I need to do.

But each time I start to worry, I remind myself: I'm just **trusting** in God and **trusting** that it all works out for the greater good. I'm going to put my best foot forward. I worry so much about the details; that's where anxiety lives. But I need to work harder not to do all that, especially when so much is out of my control.

I feel like anyone who's ever dedicated everything to their careers has always regretted it. How many executives out there on their death beds say that they would trade so much of their work success for having been there more for their kids? I'm not saying don't put effort into your career, but it's about balance. It's all about enjoying life as well as your work. The experiences you get from life are such an important tool in any profession. There's something there that can't be taught.

It's like when someone tells you that they feel the pain in a song and you really can feel the depth and emotion of their experiences and the work they create. With a lawyer, a doctor, a teacher, their emotion also comes through in everything they do. Some of your work involves things you can do by the book, but what you've been through and the depth of the life you've had also play a role. It's like the seasoning on food. All the things you've experienced have just sharpened your blade.

I've also realized that I need to make sure I keep everything I'm doing as fun as possible. There have been plenty of times that I've gotten invites to the craziest parties, and I make the choice not to go because I'd rather work on music. That's what creativity feels like when the channels are open; it's more exciting than any party in the world.

Now I cherish the moments of true pleasure, whether that's going for walks with my son, going to a Lions game in Detroit, or attending NBA games and sitting courtside. Even if I'm not at 100 percent, I've got to enjoy these moments because they're so temporary. And I find that when I make myself enjoy life and rest, I get sick way less often, and so in the long run I lose no time at all.

In what ways can you balance your work and personal life a little better?

List three things that you enjoy doing that make your life better. When's the next time you can do them?

It's never over until you're over it. The best is yet to come.

CHAPTER THIRTY
A Gift to the Future

▪ *accepting, strategizing, trying, trusting, manifesting*

MY DAD'S MOM PICKED COTTON for her job. My granddad's aunt was born a slave. That wasn't that long ago. What of them lives in me? I believe we pass along so much of ourselves to the next generation: our strengths, our fears, our pain. And if we don't work through the traumas, I believe we pass them on as well. They're undigested, and they create struggles for the next generation. That's why I feel it's so important for us to heal ourselves. It's not just so we'll have a better life but so future generations won't suffer more than they need to. By working on ourselves, we can ease their burden, too.

When my son, Noah, was born, I saw so clearly that I was connecting my family's past and future. Looking at my baby was the first time I ever felt *eternity*. I was as sure about it as two plus two equals four. The proof was right there. If, Heaven forbid, I'm not here, I'm going to be living through him. There's a comfort in realizing that this circle never ends. It's never going to end entirely just because your life ends. You will see it in your children, or if you don't have children, in the impact you have in the world through your loved ones, your work, or your friends.

From the very first minute, I saw my whole family in Noah. The first few weeks after he was born, it was like every day he looked like someone new: "Yo, Jhené, he looks like your grandpa!" Then the next day, she'd say, "Wait, he looks like my mom!" Lately, he really looks like Brett, my brother. As his face is forming, all these different sides are revealing themselves.

When Noah and I walk around and I say my affirmations, I'll add some for him, and after I sign them by saying my own name, I'll add, "Noah Anderson," like I'm signing for him, too. I treat my affirmations like my very own declaration of independence. Then I'll say, "It is done. It is done. It is done. So be it." Sometimes he seems to understand that we're doing work together to bring good fortune and full faith into the life of our family.

It's important to work on yourself because you're passing things on to your community and the circle of people that you're close with. You vibrationally rub off on people, and you never know what moments will stick with you.

My dad has always done his best to teach me the lessons he's learned. We have a deep bond that I'm reminded of at the funniest times. He used to be a real player, and I'd tease him about how he wore leather pants with silk scarves. Then, more than a decade later, I had on leather pants. My dad tapped me on the shoulder when I was walking to the stage to perform at a Lions game and said, "Hey, Leather Pants." Even though it had been two decades since I made fun of him for wearing leather pants, I knew exactly what he was talking about. We cracked up laughing.

Not long ago, my dad was bragging about having met Dave Chappelle: "Yo, man. I was just with Dave Chapelle. I was at his concert backstage. He loves your music, especially *Dark Sky Paradise*."

My dad has a tendency to exaggerate, so I said, "Yeah, it's cool you hung out with him. Okay, cool, sure. All right, Dad. Love you, peace."

About a year later, at five in the morning, I ran into Dave Chappelle hopping off a plane. It was my first time meeting him, and the first thing he said was, "Yo, man. I love your dad! I love you, too, man. I love your music. But I *love* your dad." I thought I was dreaming!

I wonder if Noah and I will surprise each other as he gets older. What I do know is that the better I am, the better it will be for Noah. I look at him and marvel at how much he's learning so quickly. He's walking and starting to say little words and playing, and he's such a happy baby. He has a golden positivity to him. It's like he's an angel, like he's a pure angel. Obviously, he can also be rambunctious. He's a messy eater. But wow, is he smart. He's healthy, he's happy, and he's beautiful, too. I enjoy holding him, especially because I know it's not going to last. I can already see more and more how he wants me to put him down so he can walk and run on his own.

Children are a reminder of how much we all need one another. We spend so much time focused on ourselves, our own concerns, our own problems, our own worlds, that we forget that we all exist as part of one larger consciousness. We do not walk through this world alone. Think about the Covid pandemic. Suddenly, we all had to stay inside our homes, fearing the same disease, going through the same global phenomenon. It's tragic, but this is one of the clearest examples of how interconnected we all are.

The point of life, I believe, is to become better for yourself and for those around you, too. With each generation, we can keep getting healthier and stronger. We must do the continuous work to become our highest selves and have an influence on other people's lives in a positive way. I hope to pass on confidence, good health, and intelligence (both emotional and educational) to my child. I hope to break generational trauma. All the work that I do now serves this purpose. It's important to do the work to be the best version of yourself, so that future generations can be born into a world that's even greater.

We are all a work in progress. We are all our greatest project. We must be conscious of how we communicate and the fact that we all communicate differently. We communicate with ourselves, others, God, and nature. We need to expand our ability not to respond but to listen. I check in with myself through meditation and through the tools I've learned in therapy. I make choices about how to spend my time, the most precious currency in life. Why spend it being angry when communication can save us and move us all forward collectively?

Life lately has been one big balancing act. Parenting has been like walking on a tightrope. There are a lot of dynamics to having a family. You have to keep perspective and have respect for your partner, respect for your child, respect for yourself. You're balancing all of those things, plus **trying** to show consideration, patience, focus, intention, attention, and gratitude. Being a parent really teaches you to prioritize certain things and be intentional with your time. I've learned that I'll probably never have it all figured out, or the second I do, things will change again.

Noah's taken to walking up and down the stairs, up and down, up and down, while I hold his hands. It's murder on my back, but it's amazing to see how much the simplest things mean to him: hopping on the curb, hopping off the curb. Being a dad tires me out, but it also gives me so much. That energy exchange is priceless.

He's been teaching me that the small wins are to be celebrated. Things that adults think are minor often give babies a great sense of joy. I **try** to see the world through his eyes as much as possible, so I can share that wonder. I feel a profound sense of happiness walking outside with him. It's the funniest thing—he holds his hand up toward the sun or a bird or a plane as though he's moving them.

"You think you control the universe, don't you?" I'll say to him, smiling.

The truth is, he actually does control the universe for me. My world revolves around him.

I recently shot a music video from Noah's point of view. The video starts with him waking up, getting a bath. It includes Jhené and me and our families. We shot moments of Noah's life. I wanted to make something that he could look back on after his granddads and grandmas are gone, so he can know how much he was loved.

In the song "On Up," I share some of the lessons I'm hoping to teach him. He is so innocent. I wonder how long that will last, and what his mother and I can do to help him stay so pure. When he was just learning how to sit up, I'd catch him when he started to fall over. It made me think of how all of us fall over sometimes and need someone to remind us to get back up. And it made me think of how one day

I might be a grandfather, how maybe after I'm gone I'll live on in some way through him.

When I see Noah smile, I see the way I lift my own eyelids up. I can see that part of me is in him. That means part of my grandma and granddad are in me, too. Even if they're not here, I like to think that spiritually they're watching over me. They're in my veins. They're in my nervous system. I think it goes that deep. It's like everyone has a sense of fluidity to them that they don't even see. That's proof of a higher power right there.

It all gets passed on. That's what I realized. And that's why it's important to be conscious of yourself and recognize, "What would I like to change about myself? Is it my fear of failure? Is it my lack of confidence? Is it my health? Is it my talent for making business deals? What do I want to pass on?"

So, ask yourself, "What do I want to correct? What do I want to change?" Because if there's something you don't want to pass on, whether it's to your descendants or to the world around you and the world that's yet to come, you've got to change your life.

My son looks at me, and we have so many similar expressions and poses. It's mind-blowing, and it's fun to watch, but it reminds me that there will come a time when he could think about how I was hesitant to try to do certain things, and that would make them all the more intimidating to him. I have to be there for him and let him know that he is his own person. And it could be as simple as giving him the confidence to go beyond me and to walk proudly with his head up.

My parents came from a different era, so they always warned me not to be too flashy, not to do anything that might get me pulled over by the cops. And I'm not saying that that isn't something to be conscious of now, because it's obviously a huge and dangerous issue for Black men in this country. But when I speak to my son about these same issues—which I will inevitably have to do, and likely sooner than I want to—I hope I can help him learn ways to be himself and not feel like he has to make himself smaller to stay safe.

My son is my motivation right now to be better in the world. I'm determined to not waste time but spend it healing myself and creating a better future for him.

As I bring this book to a close, I'd like to say that the good news is that the work is never done. Once you have your self-work routine in place, you need to keep it up.

Opportunities to apply the five practices will show up every single day, in every area of your life. At every turn, you will need to decide how you choose to **accept**, **strategize**, **try**, **trust**, and/or **manifest**. And once you **manifest** something, you'll ask yourself, "Okay, now, how does it get any better than this? What else is possible?"

You find out when you take care of yourself that you can be the biggest blessing to the world and to whoever it is you're impacting on a daily basis: your team, your family, your kids, your parents, your cousins, your community.

Whatever team or family you're part of, it's important to be the best version of yourself because you end up being the one who pushes your circle, your family, or whoever forward, as opposed to the one who weighs it down. Your work **accepting**, **strategizing**, **trying**, **trusting**, and **manifesting** is what will make you happier, and those around you happier, too, and that good work will endure for generations to come.

How can you become better not only for yourself but for others?

What generational curses do you hope to break?

What positive new traditions could you begin?

It's now or never. GO!

EPILOGUE

What Now?

THIS BOOK IS MEANT TO be read and reread. These prompts are designed to be relevant in many different situations, so you can revisit them anytime you'd like to work on yourself. I hope you'll find the five practices helpful at various stages of your life.

The next time you find yourself at an impasse, in a difficult situation with a friend or loved one, or feeling like you're facing a roadblock of some sort, I urge you to make a list:

- **Accept**
- **Strategize**
- **Try**
- **Trust**
- **Manifest**

See where and how you can apply each of these practices to help you move forward. To achieve a goal, yes, but it's about so much more than that. It's about continually readying yourself to evolve and become the next best you. That, to me, is the essence of "going higher."

You might not need to use each of these practices in each situation, or you may have already applied one and are ready for next steps. But believe me when I say that you have the power to shift the energy of the world. If you can **accept** that, you're already on your way up.

If you want to do only one thing I've talked about in this book, I'd say start by putting your energy and your attention behind whatever it is you're looking to achieve. Write affirmations and agreements in a journal. Write goals on a white board. Read them aloud. Be ready to update your goals as your life evolves.

Be intentional about how you talk. Assume that the universe is listening to you. Say to yourself, "This is how I want to dominate. This is how I want to execute. This is where I want to be in my life. And this is how I'm going to do it." Your subconscious mind is the bridge to God and the universe, the key to creating what you desire.

Celebrate the small wins as well as the big ones. A "no" today doesn't mean a "no" tomorrow. It could be a "yes" in a different way. Every person in history that I've ever looked up to has gotten knocked down so many times, has failed a lot at whatever it is they were in pursuit of doing. It only made them stronger and wiser.

It's never too late. There's always enough time. It's always going to be the right time for you.

Show gratitude, even if it's only saying thank you to those around you or looking back and saying, "Man, I'm so grateful that happened."

Remember that you have the power. Like I've said many times: You have the power of the whole universe inside you. You're a magical being, and you have what it takes to accomplish whatever your heart desires. You just have to believe it first. If you can see it, you will ultimately get a chance. If your heart and your intentions are in the right place and you're passionate, preparation will meet opportunity one way or another. I hope that when you take these practices and apply them, you'll be ready when that moment comes.

Acknowledgments

THIS BOOK IS THE FULFILLMENT of a goal I've had for a very long time. For helping me realize this dream, I'd like to thank Samantha Weiner, Sarah Passick, Ada Calhoun, and everyone else who helped make this happen, including Sarah Rountree, Melissa Rodman, Gina Navaroli, and the teams at Park Fine, Roc Nation, and Simon & Schuster. Thanks to my mother, Myra; my father, James; and my brother, Brett, for their helpful notes and love, and to Jhené Aiko for all the support while I was writing the book. And to my friend Jay Shetty, thank you so much for writing the foreword. Finally, all my love to Noah. You inspire me to make the world a better place and to always do my best.

For Further Reading

The Course of Miracles: A Philosophy of Happiness

by Peter Campelo

According to *The Course of Miracles*, the separation of man from God is an illusion. The miracle in the title refers to a "shift in perception" that could lead us to become aware of "our divine nature." The best parts of the book are the miracle stories from around the world and the focus on approaching our connection to God with pure love. Katy Perry was once touring a house of mine and pointed to this on my shelf and nodded. People who know, know.

The Secrets of the Richest Man Who Ever Lived

by Mike Murdock

This book applies more to the business aspect of life. It's about King Solomon and how he ran his empire on a technical level, from having the best counsel to the importance of confidence in motivating people. My grandma got this book for my brother, Brett, and then he gave it to me. I still use it today, especially when I'm handling my business or hiring people.

The Seven Spiritual Laws of Success

by Deepak Chopra

When I found this book at age nineteen, I felt like it was meant for me. I felt electric reading it. I've read it about four times since. One of the parts of *The Seven Spiritual Laws of Success* that I think about all the time is the Law of Least Effort. That really stuck with me, and it's about how the flow of nature, the way water flows, the way grass grows, the way the sun shines should be present in how you are when you're in your purpose, when you're in your flow. It's like how you might feel when you see an eagle in the sky, gliding on the wind.

When you're struggling, you have to ask, "Why is this so hard for me? Is this what I should be doing?" You can always look at it from different perspectives. "Am I being tested? Is this an obstacle to getting what I want or a way for me to show how much I want it? Or is this something that isn't meant for me, and I'm going against the current of the stream?"

The Alchemist

by Paulo Coelho

In *The Alchemist,* Santiago, an Andalusian shepherd boy, travels in search of treasure. In the process, he learns about listening to his heart, recognizing opportunity, and following dreams.

At one of my first shows in California, at UCLA, the promoter who booked me for the show said, "Have you ever read the book *The Alchemist*? It's changed my life, and it even helped me **manifest** booking you. A goal of mine was to book you for this show. And I'm sitting here talking to you right now. Man, you have to read this book."

He gave me his copy, and I read it. And it was life changing. I saw the world differently after I read it. It made everything I dreamed of feel more possible. And the second time I read it, I got even more out of it than I did the first time.

What You Think of Me Is None of My Business

by Terry Cole-Whittaker

A reverend wrote this book, arguing that God gave us a right to happiness, wealth, and success. The program she puts forward is about getting rid of false beliefs to discover an inner path to what we're good at and what we're destined to do. I like how the motivational tools focus on self-awareness and on looking at what you can control, not on what's outside of you.

Think Big: Take Small Steps and Build the Future You Want

by Grace Lordan

Behavioral scientist Dr. Grace Lordan looks at six areas—time, goal planning, self-narratives, other people, environment, and resilience concepts—to help come up with career strategies. I love the motivation this book gives you. It really breaks it down to the fundamentals of manifesting more in your life.

Inner Engineering: A Yogi's Guide to Joy

by Sadhguru

Sadhguru has written a lot of useful books. In this one, he tells the story of his own awakening and how he founded a humanitarian organization. The book explains how people can live a life of greater joy. It also talks about how we're all interconnected with one another and nature, and how important it is to take care of the earth.

The 48 Laws of Power

by Robert Greene

Greene offers three thousand years of the history of power via forty-eight essential laws pulled from the work of everyone from Sun Tzu to P. T. Barnum. Some of the laws are harsh ("Law 15: Crush Your Enemy Totally"), but I found it an interesting way to think about how to get in the right frame of mind to get things done.

Think Like a Monk: Train Your Mind for Peace and Purpose Every Day

by Jay Shetty

I've been on my friend Jay Shetty's podcast *On Purpose* a couple of times, and they've been a couple of the best conversations of my life. Jay uses his own experiences as a monk on an ashram to talk about getting rid of negative thoughts and bad habits, and how to become calm and deliberate. The book is incredibly soothing.

The Four Agreements: A Practical Guide to Personal Freedom

by Don Miguel Ruiz

In *The Four Agreements*, Ruiz describes a code of personal conduct he says he learned from his Toltec ancestors. For example: *Be Impeccable with Your Word, Don't Take Anything Personally, Always Do Your Best*. I especially loved how he talked about not taking things personally and just focusing on yourself: "Nothing other people do is because of you. It is because of themselves. All people live in their own dream, in their own mind; they are in a completely different world from the one we live in. When we take something personally, we make the assumption that they know what is in our world, and we try to impose our world on their world."

It's All in Your Head

by Russ

My homie Russ once told me, "There is no such thing as losing. You only lose when you stop." There is no such thing as failure, only lessons. You have to find a reason to keep going, to keep moving forward. In this book, Russ talks about how it worked for him. He realized he didn't need a major label and that what we all really need to do is take a chance on ourselves.

Getting into the Vortex

by Esther Hicks and Jerry Hicks

This book contains four guided daily meditations designed to get you into what the authors call the Vortex of Creation in four areas: General Well-Being, Financial Well-Being, Physical Well-Being, and Relationships. The Hicks family believes that, to live better, we need to come into alignment with "the Energy of our Source." I totally believe in the idea that when we meditate, we are able to tap into a higher state of being and that everything gets better for us when we do.

Ask and It Is Given

by Esther Hicks and Jerry Hicks

The first book by the authors of *Getting into the Vortex* discusses how our relationships, health issues, finances, careers, and everything else are influenced by universal laws. The book gives a simple, practical formula for how to ask for, and then how to receive, whatever we want to be, do, or have. It also argues that the closer we get to the "non-physical" elements in our lives, the less able we are to explain it.

I was referred to this book by my mom when I was heavy into knowing that I was going to be a rapper. I was still in high school, and I had just met and rapped for Kanye. I was also unhappy when things didn't go my way or when things were taking longer than expected. My mom handed me this and said it was about empowering yourself and making it happen on your own and being proactive and manifesting.

I didn't read it for a while, but then honestly, I just felt desperate. I thought, *Man, I need to be doing everything I can to make my dreams come true*. As soon as I read it, I felt like I was taking a step toward a path that I wanted to be on. I was eighteen years old when I read it. And then I ended up signing my record deal when I was nineteen.

I wanted to do music; then I wanted to start performing to get my music out into the world. Now I want to communicate some ideas that are more complicated than I can fit into a three-minute song, and so I wanted to write a book. All of that wasn't clear when I started. It was almost like one thing led to another thing, that led to another, and so on and so forth. I feel like that book helped me understand that this is how everything worthwhile comes together.